The Silent Scandal:
Stop The Toxic Attack On Our Bodies

By: Brittney Kara

Copyright Text

Published by Motivational Press, Inc.
2360 Corporate Circle
Suite 400
Henderson, NV 89074
www.MotivationalPress.com

Copyright © by Brittney Kara
All Rights Reserved

www.yourlifedetoxed.com

Edited by: Judy Sowell Lucius

No part of this book may be reproduced or transmitted in any form by any means: graphic, electronic, or mechanical, including photocopying, recording, taping or by any information storage or retrieval system without permission, in writing, from the authors, except for the inclusion of brief quotations in a review, article, book, or academic paper. The authors and publisher of this book and the associated materials have used their best efforts in preparing this material. The authors and publisher make no representations or warranties with respect to accuracy, applicability, fitness or completeness of the contents of this material. They disclaim any warranties expressed or implied, merchantability, or fitness for any particular purpose. The authors and publisher shall in no event be held liable for any loss or other damages, including but not limited to special, incidental, consequential, or other damages. If you have any questions or concerns, the advice of a competent professional should be sought.

Manufactured in the United States of America.

ISBN: 978-1-935723-93-6

Contents

Chapter 1
Our Toxic World- What They Don't Want You To Know............... 9

Chapter 2
Did You Know Your Body is a Miracle? 23

Chapter 3
Good Nutrition Starts With Real Food 57

Chapter 4
Breaking The Toxic Cycle.. 95

Chapter 5
Cleanse to Live:
How to properly detoxify your body and life 107

Chapter 6
Your Sacred Space 123

Chapter 7
Your Life Detoxed.. 131

I dedicate this book to my beautiful daughters Kayla and Kelsey, and to my husband Kellen. I would be nothing without your love and support.

I write this book in honor and memory of my dear friend, Amanda Stratt.

It is because of you all that I will never give up this fight.

Disclaimer: The information contained in this Book is intended for educational purposes only. The statements in this eBook have not been evaluated by the FDA and are not provided for use to diagnose, prescribe or treat any disease, illness or injured condition of the body, and the author, publisher, printer, or distributors accept no responsibility. Consult with a physician for all issues concerning your health.

In February of 2010 I began writing a blog called *One Angry Chick*. I became inspired to start writing the blog after having lunch with a friend and discussing the downward spiral of American health and the food industry. As we were driving in the car, something just came over me and I exclaimed, "I just wish I could wake everyone up and show them what is really going on in our world! I am so mad about all the lies being spread about our health and our well being! I need to talk about it and tell the world the truth!" My friend looked at me and said, " Wow, you are one angry chick!" That day was a pivotal day in my journey on the health and wellness crusade. I went home immediately and started writing my first blog post. After a few months of blogging, and getting some awesome feedback from my articles, it was heavy on my heart to start writing my first book. *The Silent Scandal* is all about the health crisis in America, and what each of us can do to have, what I call, *empowered health*. So, welcome to my world, welcome to my passion, and welcome to my mission to impact lives. After years of being passionate about health, doing hours of research, reading countless books and watching documentaries, I feel in my heart it is time for me to share with the world the things that have blessed my life, empowered me to make better choices about my own health, assisted me to help thousands of people, and, of course, what has made me *One Angry Chick*. This book is the culmination of the knowledge I have stored in my brain for years. I made the decision to take the time to look at what was going on around me, and make a conscious effort to change. People have asked me for years about ingredients, non-toxic products, cleansing, health, vaccines, and for nutritional advice. This is my way of giving back to more people than I could just talk to over the phone. So, what am I angry about you may be wondering? While I am not an angry person I am actually a very positive- open- and loving person, I am angry about some injustices I believe are going on in our world. I am angry that our world is so polluted; I am angry that our food is sprayed with poison, and somehow that it's legal; I am angry that obesity rates are skyrocketing; I am angry that there are deadly chemicals in our personal body care items that cause cancer; I am angry that the pharmaceutical industry has taken over our healthcare system and people think that it's normal; I am angry that I even have to worry about where and how my child's toys are made due to toxic ingredients in plastics and paints; and most of all I am angry that not that many people are educated or even talking about these subjects! This book is my mission to empower **YOU** - to take control of **your** health, and **your** life by becoming an educated consumer. I truly believe that together we can break this toxic cycle. What I want to make very clear in this book is that I will state my opinions, my personal recommendations, and suggestions for the things I believe can help you achieve optimal health, but in no way, shape or form, am I telling you, you have to do these things. It's a personal choice and commitment to be healthy everyday. No one can make that decision for you, but YOU. This book and my personal mission, is about empowering others to become educated so they can make the right decisions for themselves and their families. We have all sat by the wayside for too long, letting the media, government, and our healthcare professionals tell us what is right for our bodies, our minds, and souls. Enough is enough! Take control of your health now and know that you have the absolute power to live the healthiest, happiest, fullest life possible.

Blessings, Brittney Kara, MNLP, MH.t

Chapter 1

Our Toxic World- What They Don't Want You To Know

It used to be that our world protected us. Our environment, our land, our water, and our air made it possible for us to live. It provided us with the proper nutrients in our food, good clean water to drink and bathe in, and fresh air to fill our lungs so we could breathe. After the Industrial Revolution, all that would change forever. Our health would start declining in ways we could have never imagined. As industry progressed, our world became more and more toxic. Government agencies and large corporations began to see the profits in mass-producing goods. In a few short decades we had gone from clean to corrupt. Our air became polluted with thousands of poisons and gasses, our water became contaminated from chemicals, oil, and bacteria, and our food became a vicious trap that would cause thousands of deaths a year. Today we truly live in a very toxic world. It is almost unfathomable how many toxic substances enter our bodies on each given day. We may hear about it regularly, yet most Americans choose to ignore the reality of what is going on around us, or, they don't even understand the severity of living in such a toxic world.

On average, 600 tons of toxic chemicals are pumped into our air each year. Our water is estimated to have over 700 poisonous chemicals in it. Our food is sprayed with dozens of insecticides, herbicides, pesticides, and larvacides. It is ironic that the term "cide" in Latin means death. We are literally spraying death on our food, and then consuming it. I will talk a lot more about food in a later chapter, but just know that the food you eat everyday is covered with countless chemicals, poisons, dyes, and preservatives that are flooding your body. Our homes are beautiful little toxic sanctuaries filled with flame-retardants and chemicals that have been sprayed on our mattresses, bedspreads, carpets, and drapes. The products that we use to clean our homes are usually more dangerous than the bacteria and dirt we are trying to remove. Our clothes are laden with dyes, chemically sprayed fabrics, and synthetic materials. Our lotions and cosmetics contain carcinogenic ingredients, like parabens and sulfates that disrupt our body's functions. Even our children's toys have become something to worry about, with the plastics and paints that contain things like phthalates, (polyvinyl chloride additives) and lead in them. In fact, the United States remains one of the few developed countries to permit the import of plastic toys made with these ingredients. It seems that our environment is actually a breeding ground for disease and illness, yet little is being done about it. It sounds like a lot of negativity in one paragraph but unfortunately it is the truth. Are you getting at all concerned yet? I know I did when I first started to learn these truths.

Many of these things we can't control anymore, but there are many ways to diminish the amount of toxins you allow to come into your body everyday. There are steps you can take to remove them from your body and life. Some people don't like to hear this information because it freaks them out. It's almost easier to just put their head in the sand and pretend like none of this is going on. The truth is, we have to be aware. Our safety and lives depend on it. All of these factors affect you everyday whether you choose to be aware of it or not. My belief is, you might as well know about it, so you can *do* something about it.

I have been teased, criticized, belittled, and laughed at over the years as I shared my passion about helping others understand the concepts I am going to discuss with you in this book. There were times that it bothered me, of course, I am human and I have feelings. But, for the most part, I have felt for a long time that this is my purpose on this planet. I know now that it truly is. It is my purpose to educate others, to fight for change, and to make a positive impact on the world. There has never been a better time in our history for humankind to band together to make some serious social changes. We have so much power and potential in us, yet we get overwhelmed and bombarded by negativity, and, yes, by toxins. Through this foggy mess, we have somehow lost our way, and in turn lost our health and our power.

All of these toxic areas I discussed are vitally important to your life, because, they can actually dictate who you are, what you end up accomplishing, and the life you lead. If our bodies are not healthy we cannot function, and therefore, we cannot live the life we want, and deserve to live. Toxins affect us in many ways. They affect our cells, which in turn affects our organs, our blood, our brains, and our emotional well-being. A toxic body cannot produce the proper brain chemicals that it needs to keep our minds sharp and happy, it cannot produce healthy cells, and it cannot protect you against disease and illness.

Have you ever stopped to think why we are in such a massive health crisis in the United States? Did you know that cancer rates are higher than they have ever been in history? In fact, in the 1950's, 1 in 12 people would develop some type of cancer. It is now 1 in 2! In my seminars I always ask the room to raise their hand if they or anyone they know has ever been diagnosed with or died from cancer. Every single person in the room always has their hand up, every time. I recently lost my best friend of 25 years to Colon Cancer at the age of 33. It is beyond devastating to know that people so young are dying from these horrific diseases. Watching her and her family endure the devastating affects of cancer is something I can't put into words, but it was horrific. Cancer knows no bounds anymore and as our world becomes more toxic and our foods become more nutritionally depleted we will continue to see this disease rise. I will talk later in more detail about the cancer industry, as it's injustices are one of my many motivations for educating the world. And what about the rise in diabetes, heart disease, and autoimmune diseases? What about the increase in children that have ADHD and autism? Do you think toxicity has any part in any of these issues? The answer is, yes, it absolutely does!

The Center for Disease Control (CDC) found that people of all ages have, on average, 116 toxic chemicals in them at all times.[1] The Environmental Working Group (EWG) found an astonishing 287 toxic chemicals in the blood of newborn babies.[2] We used to think that the uterus protected the baby from the mother's impurities, but science now tells us that is not the case. Our poor children are literally being born polluted. Worse yet, is the fact that they have been soaking in a toxic environment for the first nine months of their existence. The first nine months is the most essential part of development for humans, and they are being shot in the foot before they are even exposed to greater risks in the real world. I will talk more about the health of our children in later chapters, but it is devastating and infuriating to see what is happening to our youth in this toxic world. When I first wrote this book I was pregnant with my second child. I have since given birth to a beautiful, healthy, baby girl named Kelsey. It has been my mission with both my pregnancies to focus everyday on diminishing the toxins I am exposed to in order to protect my babies. If you are a parent and reading this book, please think not only about your own health, but the health of your child, and how by implementing some of the things we are going to be discussing, you can absolutely change your child's future!

Every year there are more and more studies that come out linking toxicity to disease and illness. There is countless information out there to read, and become educated on this subject. The problem is that most people are not reading it. We all live very hectic, stressful lives, and people just do not take the time to know about the world around them. I believe that through education comes empowerment. In fact, your education is the only thing that cannot be taken away from you. Knowledge truly is power. My goal with this book is for it to be a guide for you to start your journey of empowering yourself to become healthier, happier, and more balanced.

People often say to me, "how come the government isn't doing anything to stop this if the problem is so bad?" My answer is always the same: The government is a big, if not the biggest part of the toxic problem. It used to be we could put 100% faith, trust, and support in our government officials. We know today that is not the case. Washington has become a very corrupt, and should I say, toxic place. Greed is the biggest factor contributing to the problems we are facing as a society. The truth is that the government does not want us to be healthy. In fact, they make a lot of money from us being very sick, overweight, and depressed. Our government, media, healthcare system, and pharmaceutical industry in the U. S. are entirely controlled by greed and corruption. The FDA, in my opinion, is one of the scariest institutions we have. They continually put drugs on the market that are barely tested, contain highly damaging ingredients to the body, and are promoted as "healthcare". The bottom line is that we don't really have healthcare in this country anymore; we have "sick care". I work with a lot of doctors, some western medical doctors, and some eastern and holistic doctors. All of my doctor friends say that the quickest place to get sick or die is in a hospital. How sad is that? I will show you later how that is absolutely a true statement.

There are certain governmental agencies, lobbyists, and investors that are running our world and making the decisions for our health. It is not an accident that our food is filled with junk, our water is polluted, our air is deadly to breathe, or that we are bombarded with drugs and medicines to put a band-aid on these issues. This is all part of a very specific plan, designed to have control of Americans. You might be thinking that I sound like some sort of conspiracy theorist by saying this, but unfortunately it is not just a theory, it is truth. You don't have to take my word for it though, please do your research and formulate your own opinion. There is loads of information, documentaries, and writings out there that reveal what is truly going on in our government behind our backs. In the back of this book I have created, what I call, an **Educated Consumers Empowerment Guide**, or **ECEG** for short, so that you can start to research and learn for yourself the things I am going to discuss with you. Although I am not going to go too deeply into my personal political philosophies in this book, I am going to share with you information about the U. S. government that I believe is very important for your health and safety. Some information stated in this book is my personal belief or opinion, so I strongly recommend you doing your own research as well, and forming your own conclusions about what is happening. My belief is that when you start to search for the truth you will be shocked at what you find!

One of the biggest toxic problems in America besides our food is our drug addiction. I am not speaking about illegal drugs, which, of course, are a problem too; I am speaking about prescription drugs and the horrific effects they are placing on our health. It has become acceptable and mainstream to be on a plethora of prescription drugs. Most people don't even know or ask what or why they need certain prescriptions. We have been taught and programmed that doctors are all knowing and Godlike. We must obey what they tell us, because they are educated and we are not. The truth is that most doctors are barely educated on the mass amounts of drugs they shell out daily to patients because they lack the time to do the research. Plus, most of their continuing education is paid for and offered by the pharmaceutical companies. Pharmaceutical companies distribute drugs like candy, and there are lots of perks for the doctors who participate. A lot of the new drugs don't even have proper research behind them before they are shoved out into the market. The FDA is not an organization that I trust, and they have proven time and time again to be wrong with their studies and findings on health.

How many medications have been pulled off the market because of their deadly side effects? There are too many to even count. Do you know how many people die each year from complications due to modern medicine? According to the report done by a group of several M.D's, "Death by Medicine", there were 783,936 deaths in 2003.[3] That is the equivalent of six jumbo jet crashes happening each day for a whole year! If six jumbo jets crashed, even all on one day, it would be world news! We would think the world was coming to an end and that terrorists must have been involved. Yet no one is talking about this healthcare statistic. This is happening to us, right here, right now. According to Natural News, prescription drugs are 16,400% more deadly than terrorists. [4] I bet you won't see that statistic on the news either. Well I wonder why not? If our government and medical community were really trying to protect us, why are they not regulating this problem? Why is the mass public not being educated on this issue? Why are there not press conferences about this every day? Why are people not searching for a solution to this epidemic? The answer to all of these questions is greed. The pharmaceutical industry is a multi-billion dollar a year industry, and the sad truth is, there is no money in healthy people that don't need drugs. I will discuss more about drugs in Chapter 2.

"The best six doctors anywhere,
And no one can deny it,
Are sunshine, water, rest, and air,
Exercise and diet.
These six will gladly you attend
If only you are willing
Your mind they'll ease
Your will they'll mend
And charge you not a shilling. "

~Nursery rhyme quoted by Wayne Fields, *What the River Knows***, 1990**

Personally I rarely ever go to a medical doctor. I do my annual female check-ups, and that is it. I would much rather go to a holistic practitioner, get acupuncture, go get reiki, and take homeopathic remedies than take one step into a traditional MD's office. The funny thing is I rarely ever get sick. Most people I know that go to the doctor regularly to get their antibiotics, prescriptions, and pharmaceutical drugs are always sick. The healthiest people I know rarely go to the doctor. I'm not saying you should stop going to the doctor, I'm saying that if you become educated enough about your own body and what your choices are for health, then maybe you would be better equipped at handling some of the issues that life throws at you. If my arm gets severed and I need medical attention, then I will, obviously, go seek a doctor's care. If I have a cough, or a headache, or an upset tummy, I will not run to my doctor to get drugs, but a lot of people do. That is the result of a toxic world that is uneducated about their bodies. We have so much more control than we think over our health and ourselves, but we have put our faith into organizations and people that do not have our best interest in mind. They want us to be sick, and they want our minds to be so polluted and filled with other nonsense that we never question their authority.

According to the "Death By Medicine" study thousands of medical records were researched to examine this exact issue. Here is what they found:

> "The United States spends $282 billion annually on deaths due to medical mistakes, or iatrogenic deaths. And that's a conservative estimate; only a fraction of medical errors are reported, according to the study. Actual medical mistakes are likely to be 20 times higher than the reported number because doctors fear retaliation for those mistakes. The American public heads to the doctor's office or the hospital time and again; oblivious of the alarming danger they're heading into. The public knows that medical errors occur, but they assume that errors are unusual, isolated events. Unfortunately, by accepting conventional medicine, patients voluntarily continue to walk into the leading cause of death in America." [5]

The Nutrition Institute of America, a non-profit, non-partisan organization who has been leading the way to educate the public about heath issues for over 30 years, also had similar findings.

> "New information has been presented showing the degree to which Americans have been subjected to injury and death by medical errors. The results of seven years of research reviewing thousands of studies conducted by the NIA now show that medical errors are the number one cause of death and injury in the United States.
> According to the NIA's report, over 784,000 people die annually due to medical mistakes. Comparatively, the 2001 annual death rate for heart disease was 699,697 and the annual death rate for cancer was 553,251. Over 2.2 million people are injured every year by prescription drugs alone and over 20 million unnecessary prescriptions for antibiotics are prescribed annually for viral infections. The report also

shows that 7.5 million unnecessary medical and surgical procedures are performed every year and 8.9 million people are needlessly hospitalized annually. Based on the results of NIA's report, it is evident that there is a pressing need for an overhaul of the entire American medical system. The findings, described as a "revelation" by Martin Feldman, MD, who helped to uncover the evidence, are the product of the first comprehensive studies on iatrogenic incidents. Never before has any study uncovered such a massive amount of information with regard to iatrogenesis. Historically, only small individual partial studies have been performed in this area. Carolyn Dean, MD, a physician and author who also helped to uncover the findings said, "I was completely shocked, amazed, and
dismayed when I first added up all the statistics on medical death and saw how much allopathic medicine has betrayed us." [6]

So how did this happen to us? Why are we so sick, overweight, and depressed? More importantly, what can we do about it? The first step to change any situation is, first recognizing there is a problem. If you have read this far and don't think that any of this affects you and there is no problem, then this book is especially for you. I am also speaking to the person that wants to learn about their health, knows they live in a toxic world, and wants to do something about it. I am speaking to every woman, man, and child that wants to live a long, healthy, vibrant life.

"He who takes medicine and neglects to diet wastes the skill of his doctors." ~ Chinese Proverb

The reality is, this happened to us because we let it happen. We were too busy watching our reality shows, reading our gossip magazines, watching CNN (which in my world stands for Constantly Negative News), and running around like chickens with our heads chopped off, so that we can make enough money to drive our SUVs, wear designer clothes, and "live the American Dream". In the process, we put our lives in the hands of people who do not have our best interests in mind. We let advertisements and media dictate what we are going to put in and on our bodies. We have lost our minds, our individuality, our health, and most importantly, we have lost a huge amount of our freedom.

Fortunately, now that you have begun to educate yourself on these matters, you have an opportunity to change your situation and to make better choices. One of my mentors and gurus Gandhi said, "Be the change you wish to see in the world." I live by that statement everyday. There is a beautiful world out there filled with health, vitality, and longevity; we just have to push through the filth to get there. You have to want to fight for your life, literally!

"In minds crammed with thoughts, organs clogged with toxins, and bodies stiffened with neglect, there is just no space for anything else." - Alison Rose Levy [7]

Chapter 2

Did You Know Your Body is a Miracle?

Your body is a miracle, literally. Did you know our bodies are comprised of 100 trillion cells? That our cells regenerate at 1 billion cells per minute? Did you know that our body is constantly breaking down and metabolizing nutrients, our immune systems are constantly warding off disease and illness, and our heart is pumping 72 times per minute, 100,00 times a day, and almost 38 million times a year? Each time it beats it pumps 2.4 ounces of blood, therefore it pumps 1.3 gallons per minute, 1,900 gallons per day, and almost 700,000 gallons per year! That is pretty incredible for a 10 ounce little pump! Heart Disease is reported as the leading cause of deaths in America. It is really the second, but no one is advertizing the deaths from medical malpractices as we discussed earlier, so we will just say it is the leading cause. With heart disease on the rise, don't you think people would want to take good care of their precious little pump? Shouldn't we know more about it and how to protect it, since it does so much for us? Apparently we don't, because most Americans are living a lifestyle that is devastating to heart health.

"The longer I live the less confidence I have in drugs and the greater is my confidence in the regulation and administration of diet and regimen." - John Redman Coxe, 1800

The heart is just one organ in your body. While it is extremely important, there are many other parts of your body that, without their functions, you either can't live, or you can't live a quality life.

Our bodies are meant to detoxify against impurities and toxins that come in. We have a liver, a colon, the kidneys, the digestive system and gall bladder to remove waste. The problem is that because our world is so toxic, and we do not take care of our bodies through proper nutrition, our organs start to become overloaded and shut down. Your liver is your main detoxifier. Everything that enters your body gets filtered through it. You can imagine that over time, the liver could become dirty and overloaded, if not taken care of properly. How many times have you stopped to think about how you have been treating your liver? Seriously, think about that for a second. When is the last time you took the time to check in and see if your liver was healthy, or if you were treating it properly? You see, our bodies do so much for us everyday, yet we take it for granted. We take health for granted until it is too late and it is gone. Then we pray to get it back. Why not just take the time to realize what our bodies do for us, take care of them, and be grateful every day? This would save so much time, money, and heartache. It is beyond heartbreaking watching someone you love get sick and suffer when their bodies shuts down from lack of care. I don't believe people want to make themselves sick, I just believe they don't know better. Unless you go into a specialized field for health, this may be the first time you are hearing some of this information.

Besides your vital organs, you have tissues and glands that are all made up of cells. It all starts with the cell, all 100 trillion of them! One of my health mentors, Jim Rhodes, a well-known nutritionist and speaker taught me that we have more cells than all the stars in the Milky Way galaxy. That is pretty incredible to think about. Have you ever wondered how they work or what they do for you everyday? Most people never stop to even think about it, but this is very important for us to understand. We must first build healthy cells in order to build healthy organs, tissues, and glands. Our cells are exposed to, and absorb, all the toxins and chemicals that we breathe, drink, and eat. So, therefore, if you choose to put toxic things in your body, on top of the environmental exposure we have everyday, you will produce toxic unhealthy cells, which will, in turn, produce toxic unhealthy organs, tissues, and glands. It's that simple, that black and white. The factors that contribute to our cells' functions are not just solely based on what we choose to do everyday to our bodies, but it is also extremely affected by our environment.

In our environment there are things called free radicals. Free radicals are like atoms gone bad. They are constantly floating around us at all time, and they attack the structure and health of our cells. Free radicals are created from smoking, pollution, poisons, and fried foods. Free radicals are also a by-product of normal metabolism. As the body uses oxygen the by-products cause oxidative damage to the cell. Free radicals are associated with the increased risk of many chronic diseases, including cancer. So how can we protect ourselves against these little buggers if they are a normal part of our environment and bodily functions?

We can protect ourselves by the use of antioxidants. There are different types of antioxidants that combat free radicals and help reduce their damaging effects. Vitamin C, carotenes, and vitamin E are a few antioxidants that support the battle against free radicals. Our cells need to have vitamins and minerals flooding them on a daily basis to help protect against these negative forces. There are many vitamins and minerals that the body needs everyday to function properly. Your body needs ninety essential nutrients daily to construct a perfect cell and to help the body function properly. Sixty of these nutrients are minerals; thirty of them are a combination of vitamins, amino acids, and fatty acids. We will be going into detail about vitamins and minerals in the chapter on food. The other vital thing that we need to maintain proper health is water.

Getting enough good water in your body daily is one of the main essential keys to a healthy life.

Water Does a Body Good

Your body is primarily made up of water. An adult body is about 70% water, and at the time of birth, a baby's birth weight is about 80% water. Your blood is mostly water, along with your muscles, lungs, and even your brain. Your body needs water to help nutrients travel to your organs, and to regulate your body temperature. Water also transports oxygen to your cells, removes waste, and protects your joints and organs. Let's just say that water is extremely important for you. Yet most people don't drink enough water.

I talk to people all the time that I am coaching and I ask them how much water they drink. Sometimes people will actually say less than a glass a day because they don't like water! That is like saying you don't like anything about yourself, because YOU are mostly water! Drinking enough water, and the right kind of water, is vital to our lives. We don't have a choice; we have to drink water, period. The best kind of water to drink is structured water. This water is alkaline, and also has minerals in it. Structured water is easier for your cells to absorb, and gives your body the proper hydration that is needs. **(See your ECEG)**

A lot of Americans get their water intake sadly from sodas, coffee, juices, or other beverages that are mixed with water. Although these caffeinated beverages do contain water, it causes the body to excrete more water than it actually is taking in. This results in the body having less fluid than it began with, and can lead to health problems over time such as constipation, bladder infections, or different skin issues.

Caffeine does appear naturally in certain things that are actually good for our health. There are small amounts of caffeine in green tea and dark chocolate for instance, which are both very good for health. The small amount of caffeine in them is not equal to the overall health benefits they provide. I am not anti- caffeine, I am anti the over abundance of caffeine which most Americans drink. Because we are so bombarded with caffeinated beverages, we forget to even consume a minimum amount of water everyday. That is not okay. It also can depend on the amount and the regularity of the caffeine going into the system that can be really harmful. Too much caffeine can actually rob the body of water and dehydrate the cells.

According to Dr. Batmaghelidj, who is an author and health expert, there is a very important balance of water and salt in the body. This balance, if disrupted, can lead to different types of disease and illness. He believes that most of the imbalances and sickness in the body is from dehydration. He says, "You're not sick, you're thirsty. Don't treat thirst with medication." His research on water and caffeine in the body states this:

> "Coffee, or rather CAFFEINE, is what will stimulate the adrenal glands to release adrenaline. CAFFEINE will also cause the body to release its own stored energy it has for an emergency. When the stored energy is released, the body will borrow what it needs to put the energy back into its emergency system so it can react to another emergency. CAFFEINE will cause the body to cannibalize off itself. Every cell in the body needs water and salt to maintain healthy cells that will work together to keep a person in good health." [8]

Caffeine can stimulate and weaken the adrenal glands, liver, and it irritates the gallbladder. It increases cortisol levels, which is the hormone responsible for weight gain. Too much caffeine consumption can put fat around the abdominal organs. It also increases adrenaline. All in all, too much caffeine is not good for us, and we should monitor our consumption of it closely.

Water is the best beverage we can consume, and we need to consume it daily. The best measure of how much water your body needs is to take your current body weight, divide it by two, and that is how much water you should be consuming each day in ounces. For example, if you weigh 130 pounds you should be consuming about 65 ounces of water per day. Bottom line is, we must have water to live and to take care of our bodies properly. Dr. Batmaghelidj's research indicates that the body can be healed from these aliments and diseases just by drinking more water. Here is a list of things he says can be cured and prevented from drinking enough water.

>Water prevents and helps to cure heartburn.
>Water prevents and helps to cure arthritis.
>Water prevents and helps to cure back pain.
>Water prevents and helps to cure angina.
>Water prevents and helps to cure migraines.
>Water prevents and helps to cure colitis.
>Water and salt prevent and helps to cure asthma.
>Water prevents and helps to cure high blood pressure.
>Water prevents and helps to cure early adult-onset diabetes.
>Water lowers blood cholesterol

To read more on Dr. Batmaghelidj's work go to www.watercure.com

Several of these alignments listed above are among the top grossing prescription drugs on the market. Does your doctor ever ask you how much water you're drinking, or talk about the effects of dehydration before they write the prescription? They probably do not. Take a look at the statistics from the CDC about the high blood pressure epidemic in the U. S.

>-About one out of three U. S. adults—31.3%—has high blood pressure.
>-High blood pressure is a major risk factor for heart

disease, stroke, congestive heart failure, and kidney disease.

-High blood pressure was listed as a primary or contributing cause of death for 326,000 Americans in 2006.

-In 2010, high blood pressure will cost the United States $76.6 billion in health care services, medications, and missed days of work.

-About 70% of those with high blood pressure and took medication had their high blood pressure controlled. The control rate was 46.6% among all hypertensive patients.

-25% of American adults have pre-hypertension - blood pressure numbers that are higher than normal, but not yet in the high blood pressure range. Pre-hypertension raises your risk for high blood pressure. (9)

It seems so simple, right? Just drink more water and your body can do what it needs to do to be healthy. So why don't we just drink more water to help with these issues? We don't because we are not taught to. You may be thinking it sounds too simple and couldn't work, but what if it does and we have all just been lied to about our bodies and what we need to 'get better'. When the pharmaceutical industry took over our healthcare system, all of the simplistic and natural education about our bodies and health went by the wayside. There is no money in people drinking water for health, and that is why it is not discussed as much as it should be. I think we all know we should drink more water, but most people don't really understand the dire consequences of not doing so. If we did, I believe people would drink more water without question. However everything comes back to money at some point, and a recent article published by Natural News discussed the CEO of Nestle, the largest food and beverage company in the world, talking about how water should and may be controlled in the future. (10) The food and beverage industry is definitely a force to be worried about, but before we go down that path let's take a closer look at an industry that has so much control over our health these days. An industry that is not only profitable, but also poisonous; the pharmaceutical industry.

The 21st Century Drug Dealers

Pharmaceuticals are big business. Doctors are under strict guidelines to prescribe drugs to "help" with the different health issues we are facing. The problem is, these drugs cause more harm than good. All of these problems could be diminished and even eradicated by going back to nature- lots of water, good nutrition, and cleansing. The pharmaceutical industry is one of the most profitable industries in the world. According to Pharmacy Times,

> "Drug sales in the United States grew by 5.1% in 2009, reaching $300.3 billion. Although this was a marked improvement from the record low growth in 2007 and 2008, 2009 sales remained relatively meager compared with the double-digit gains seen a few years ago.[1-4] To put it in perspective, the growth rate of drug sales in the United States has dropped below 5% only 3 times in the past 50 years.[5] Antipsychotics were the highest grossing class of medications, with sales of $14.6 billion, followed by lipid regulators, which dropped 1% to $14.3 billion. Lipid regulators were also the most commonly prescribed medications, growing by 4% to an estimated 211 million prescriptions. Lipitor, manufactured by Pfizer, was the single highest grossing medication in 2009, although revenue actually decreased by approximately 3% to just over $7.5 billion. The third highest class in sales in 2009 - proton pump inhibitors - experienced a 1% decline in sales but a 5% increase in prescriptions dispensed.[1] The shift to less expensive generic alternatives may account for the loss in revenue despite the growth in prescription volume. Antidepressants were ranked fourth in total sales, growing by 4% to $9.9 billion." [11]

It's sickening to me that all of these issues could be resolved naturally without medications, under the care and supervision of the appropriate health professional, using the foundation of good health: clean food, clean water, and exercise. It's not rocket science, but for some reason our health is the most misunderstood concept right now.

For example, garlic is a powerful, natural, substance that can help the body heal from a multitude of health issues. Besides being a natural antibiotic, garlic can help to lower high blood pressure. Throughout history garlic has been used in herbal medicine for curing almost everything from the common cold to the plague. Recent studies have shown that aged garlic extract can be used as a replacement for conventional drugs that reduce hypertension and blood pressure. Aged garlic extract (AGE), a dietary supplement, is a concentrated form of organic garlic. Unlike fresh garlic, the aged garlic extract does not have the odor. It is even higher in antioxidant content than the fresh garlic. In some preclinical studies, AGE has been found effective in preventing atherosclerosis (hardening of blood vessels), and protecting against cardiovascular disease. It also increases blood circulation and boosts immunity. Do you or someone you love have issues with high blood pressure? Are you wondering why your doctor has never mentioned AGE to you or anything natural for that matter? You should absolutely be wondering these things and begin asking your healthcare professionals these investigative questions. If you are on medications, what do you have to lose by trying natural remedies that have been around for thousands of years? Most people have to deal with all the debilitating side effects of the drugs they are on, just to get rid of the small problem that they began with. Wouldn't it be amazing to be able to diminish your symptoms naturally, save money on your prescription drug costs, and allow your body to function as the miracle it was intended to be? That is my goal for every human on this planet. When we have the knowledge it gives us more choices, and with more choices comes more freedom.

It seems so simple to take care of our health naturally. Yet, we don't treat our bodies properly, and usually someone's health has to hit rock bottom before they start doing this type of research and questioning what they have been told. Let's take a look at why this may be. There are several reasons I think this is the case.

> 1. Lack of Knowledge - People are not properly taught about their bodies and how to maintain optimal health and wellbeing.
> 2. Lack of Time -We all lead very hectic busy lives and most people aren't willing to take the time to educate themselves.
> 3. Lack of Responsibility -We have a microwave mentality of quick fixes and we focus on paying attention to material needs more than we do our health.

Your Six Million Dollar Investment

In my seminars I use the car analogy a lot to talk about our bodies. Most Americans take better care of their cars than they do their own bodies. We get our oil changed, our tires rotated, our engines checked, and we put the right fuel in our vehicle so that it runs properly. I believe we do this for three reasons. First, cars are an investment and they are expensive to fix if we don't take care of them. Second, we need our cars to run properly so we can go from place to place with ease to live our lives. Third, we understand the concept of prevention, and we know we need to stay up to date with our check-ups so that the vehicle can last longer.

Your body is no different than your car. In fact, it is much more important to take care of your body than your car. Each of our human bodies is estimated to be worth six million dollars! That's right, your body right now, is that big of an investment to you! Yet we fail to take care of it properly. We don't change our oil, meaning most people do not cleanse their bodies, we don't make exercise and fitness a priority, and we don't put the proper fuel in our tanks, in the form of good nutrition and fluids. But why not? Our bodies are our vehicles to get us through life. If our bodies breakdown we cannot function and live to our full potential. If you drove a six million dollar car, how would you treat it? More importantly, how are you treating your six million dollar investment right now?

We have been programmed by the media, our upbringings, our work environments, and even our government that our material possessions - the car we drive, the house we live in, and the clothes we wear - are more important than what is really our number one asset; our health. If you have money but you don't have your health, at some point you will lose all your money trying to get your health back. Your health is **the most important** asset in your life. Treat it that way.

Besides your heart, your immune system is, in my opinion, the second most important asset your body has. Your immune system is your number one fighting force against the common cold or cancer. If you don't take care of your immune system, it cannot take care of you when you need it. The immune system is something that doctors are still trying to learn more about, as it is a remarkable aspect of the body, and can be highly complicated. I think of our immune systems as our little soldiers out there fighting for us everyday against all the bad stuff. Our immune systems are constantly at work warding off disease and illness, or trying to. If our soldiers have been fed and are well rested then we can put up a good fight, but, if they are tired, hungry and weak, then we sometimes fall victim to the various health issues that can turn into disease and illness. So how do you keep your immune system up and ready to fight? The answer is to keep your body in an alkaline state.

The body is meant to function in a state of alkalinity. There is a pH balance in your body just like there is one for water. It is actually the exact same scale. Since we just learned that our bodies are mostly water, this would make sense. The human body functions best at the 7.35-7.45 rages. Anything below 7.35 is considered acidic. Your body becomes acidic from all the things we have been discussing. It becomes acidic from air, food, water, and stress. If we put the wrong foods or beverages into our bodies, our pH goes from alkaline to acidic and we may start to not feel well. Some of the signs of an acidic body are low energy, frequent sicknesses, headaches, high stress levels, anxiety, and even depression. Foods and beverages can almost instantaneously turn the body acidic. The worst part about this is that when the body is acidic, the immune system becomes compromised, and we start to become susceptible to disease and illness. When the body is acidic our soldiers can't fight for us.

Cancer is the result of the body being too acidic. Cancer cells cannot live in an alkaline body, they cannot thrive and therefore they die off. If people could just understand this simple concept we could literally stop one of the biggest killers on the planet! But there is a reason that most doctors, and our western medical world do not talk about this. The truth is, cancer is big business. I will come back to this in a minute, but let me first explain how what I just stated is true. Each of our cells takes in oxygen, glucose, and different nutrients, while trying to excrete toxins. Our cells are protected by the immune system. As I just mentioned, when the body gets acidic the immune system starts to get overpowered by the toxins and the cell is unable to take in the oxygen that it needs. This is when problems start to occur. According to my dear friend, Dr. Tony O'Donnell, in his book, *Miracle Super Foods that Heal*, he states:

> "When the cells don't get enough of the oxygen they need to produce energy, they ferment blood sugar (glucose) for energy instead. But when that blood sugar breaks down into lactic acid, it raises the acidity-the pH-level- of your body... your body needs an alkaline environment for all its metabolic processes. Healthy tissues are always oxygenated. When you gradually increase your body's alkalinity, you simultaneously increase the oxygen levels in all your or-

gans and tissues. If you keep your body at an alkaline pH level of 7.4, you'll stop the growth of diseased cells by literally starving them to death and you'll put your body in a condition for good health. Remember diseased cells' only source of life is energy from fermentation."

Dr. O'Donnell goes on to state
"an alkaline body is death to cancer. At an alkaline pH slightly above 7.6, cancer cells stop growing and replicating. At pH 8.5 cancer cells die." [12]

Dr. O'Donnell is one of my mentors and a gift to this world. He is an international speaker, holistic nutritionist, a nutritional formulator, and an author of many amazing books on health. His passion lies in teaching people how to heal their bodies naturally through super foods and cleansing. He dedicated his life to this cause after watching his beloved fiancé die of cancer undergoing traditional medical intervention. May God bless her soul and her courage for her fight. Dr. O'Donnell formulates phenomenal health products that help the body address many of the issues we have been discussing. I use his healthy greens and healthy fruits in our house everyday. Dr. Tony O'Donnell is an absolute genius when it comes to health. You can learn more about Dr. O'Donnell and his products by going to www.radientgreens.com

I mentioned earlier that I recently lost my best friend to Colon Cancer. Before I move on to the next section I need to express how emotionally devastating it was for me to watch her endure what she did as she battled this disease. I have known about the inner workings of the cancer industry for many years, but watching someone you love become another number in their system was one of the hardest, if not the hardest, experience of my life. The things that I believe could have saved her life are either not legal here in the US, as I will explain below, or were just too expensive to have access to. Like so many other innocent people she was left with limited options based on what was handed to her by the Big Pharma Industry. I will miss her forever and will never get over what she had to endure. It is in her honor and memory that I will continue to do everything I can to change what I am about to discuss with you.

The Business of Cancer

When the cells become acidic they become susceptible to cancer and are over taken by its power. The minute our cells can't absorb the oxygen needed, it is over. Cancers thrive in an acidic body, and that is why once you get cancer, it spreads very quickly. Cancers feed off acidic foods such as sugars, white breads, meats, sodas, and alcohol. That's why Americans have so much cancer, because our diet is the perfect breeding ground for it. We are literally feeding the cancer cells in our bodies everyday, helping them get stronger and stronger until it is too late and the cancer takes over. This is the sorry state of American health, and the S.A.D (Standard American Diet), which is really heartbreakingly sad. This problem is now rapidly spreading from America to all over the world. We are seeing the same kind of cancer statistics in Europe as well.

According to Patrick Rattigan, a British ND,

> "The cancer business is second only, in size, to its big brother, petrochemicals. In the 20 years from 1970 to 1990, in the USA alone, the cancer business was worth an estimated 1 trillion dollars ($1,000,000,000,000). [2] If the same percentage of the overall disease bill applies in Britain as in the US, the current expenditure on cancer will be 3 to 6 billion pounds per year. With these kind of amounts involved it is quite understandable why the drug/radiation/scalpel/vivisection cancer cartel have maintained a constant, ruthless campaign to suffocate,

at birth, any and all attempts to introduce rational therapeutic regimes to deal with the species-threatening plague. "

"Cancer is, above all else, a nutritional problem. The lethal British diet of meat, dairy produce, eggs, refined carbohydrates, common salt and synthetics, with token amounts of fruit, vegetables and whole wheat bread - all saturated with pesticides - is a recipe for a vast range of maladies, cancer included. 1999 will see 700,000,000 drug prescriptions dished out by British doctors: a deluge of vaccines, antibiotics, analgesics, steroids, antipyretics, anti-inflammatory... all add up to a huge onslaught on the body's immune defenses. Acute diseases, the body's efforts to regain health, are being continually suppressed by allopathic treatment." [13]

Wow, startling isn't it? When I started researching this stuff years ago, I literally couldn't sleep for days. I was so distraught by all the research out there unveiling the truth about the cancer industry. Yet again, no one is talking about it. This issue is purposely not front-page news. I hope by now you can see why I am just a little bit upset. Not only did someone I dearly love pass away but to know that there is an industry out their stifling information that could save these people's lives is just unfathomable. The more I researched and the deeper I dug the worse it got. Bottom line is there will never be a 'Cure for Cancer' in this country or the world for that matter until we as a people overthrow the pharmaceutical control and get our power back.

Research shows that less than one-fourth of doctors surveyed routinely ask their patients about their dietary habits. We know that cancer is a nutritional and toxic problem, yet doctors don't even ask those types of questions. It is absolutely absurd and corrupt. Are you feeling sick yet? Do you feel lied to, angry, and abused? Do you have someone in your life that you love and you watched him or her die of cancer? Did any of the doctors ever mentioned anything to you about alkalinity, or that cancer cells could be killed that way? Are you getting angry yet like I am? Good, you should. We have every right to be pissed off. We have every right to say something about it. We have every right to fight for justice! Read on, it gets even better. Here is what some medical doctors have to say about this industry and their experience in it. Many MDs have left this industry and gone the holistic route because, morally, they knew what is happening is wrong, very wrong. Here are just a few quotes from some of the medical doctors that have left the traditional Cancer institution.

> "To the cancer establishment, a cancer patient is a profit center. The actual clinical and scientific evidence does not support the claims of the cancer industry. Conventional cancer treatments are in place, as the law of the land because they pay, not heal, the best. Decades of the politics-of-cancer-as-usual have kept you from knowing this, and will continue to do so unless you wake up to this reality."
>
> John Diamond, MD & Lee Cowden MD

> "We have a multi-billion dollar industry that is killing people, right and left, just for financial gain. Their idea of doing research is to see whether two doses of this poison is better than three doses of that poison."
>
> Glenn A. Warner, MD, former head of the immunotherapy department of the Tumor Institute

> "Chemotherapy is an incredibly lucrative business for doctors, hospitals, and pharmaceutical companies... The medical establishment wants everyone to follow the same exact protocol. They don't want to see the chemotherapy industry go under, and that's the number one obstacle to any progress in oncology."
>
> Dr. Warner, M.D.

"As a retired physician, I can honestly say that unless you are in a serious accident, YOUR BEST CHANCE OF LIVING TO A RIPE OLD AGE IS TO AVOID DOCTORS AND HOSPITALS AND LEARN NUTRITION, HERBAL MEDICINE AND OTHER FORMS OF NATURAL MEDICINE. Almost all drugs are toxic and are designed only to treat symptoms and not to cure anyone. Most surgery is unnecessary. In short, our mainstream medical system is hopelessly inept and/or corrupt. THE TREATMENT OF CANCER AND DEGENERATIVE DISEASES IS A NATIONAL SCANDAL. The sooner you learn this, the better off you will be."

Dr. Allan Greenberg

Modern medicine is not a science. Doctors, medical researchers and drug companies like to persuade all present and potential consumers of health-care that medicine is a science and has advanced far beyond the mystical incantations and witch doctor remedies of the past. But modern medicine is not a science and modern clinicians and medical researchers are not scientists. Modern clinicians may use scientific techniques but in the way that they treat their patients they are still quacks...Too many modern doctors neither cure nor care. The savage truth is that most medical research is organized, paid for, commissioned or subsidized by the drug industry (and the food, tobacco and alcohol industries). Ignorance has become commonplace."

Dr. Vernon Coleman's article
"Modern Medicine is not a Science"

There has been much debate between the traditional medical field and the natural medical field about the use of vitamin C to treat and kill cancer. I am hoping by this point you are leaning more to the natural side of the debate. I personally would much rather pump my body full of massive amounts of vitamin C if I had cancer than to have my body flooded with chemotherapy. The sad thing is most people are not being made aware of this research. In the Natural Medical and Integrative Medical field many people are fighting cancer with high doses of vitamin C. Here is what ***An Oasis of Healing –A Comprehensive Cancer Center,*** had to say on the subject and the research they have pertaining to High Dose Vitamin C Therapy,

> "Cancer cells, unlike healthy human cells are both defective and primitive.
> Not only are they unable to use oxygen to metabolize glucose into energy, they are either lacking or completely deficient in many enzymes that normal cells have in abundance. One such enzyme is "catalase," which transforms oxygen and water into hydrogen peroxide, and vice versa. High doses of ascorbic acid (Vitamin C) result in the production of peroxides in and around cells. Healthy cells use the hydrogen peroxide for certain metabolic needs and the excess is converted into water and oxygen (good stuff).
> Since cancer cells have very little catalase, they are unable to convert the hydrogen peroxide into water and oxygen and consequently are oxidized and killed. So vitamin C is "good" for healthy cells and "bad" for cancer cells. The National Institute of Health (NIH), the National Cancer Institute (NCI) and the Food and Drug Administration (FDA) have finally confirmed the research findings that Linus Pauling, PhD, Hugh Riordan, MD and many other scientists and physicians over the past few decades have conducted regarding the therapeutic utility of treating cancer with vitamin C. The NIH study confirms in vitro, the hypotheses described by Riordan et al in "Intravenous Ascorbate as a Chemotherapeutic and Biologic Response Modifying Agent":
> 1. Tumor cells are more susceptible to the effects of high-dose, ascorbate-induced peroxidation products because of a relative catalase deficiency.

2. Concentrations of ascorbate high enough to kill tumor cells can be achieved in humans.
Neil H. Riordan PhD. commented on the study, "It is gratifying to have our research on vitamin C and cancer confirmed by scientists at the prestigious National Institutes of Health." [14]

There has been lots of researcher that indicates diets high in vitamin C can significantly reduce the risk of many types of cancer, such as throat, stomach, mouth, and pancreatic cancers. Vitamin C has also been found effective in reducing breast, rectum and cervical cancers. The best way to get this nutrient into your body is to eat fresh raw foods that are high in vitamin C whenever you can. Here is a list of foods that are highly concentrated with this powerful vitamin.

Tomatoes and *fresh* tomato juice (I am not talking about processed juices like V8)

Cabbage	Collard Greens Kale
Cauliflower	Kiwi
Broccoli	Mango
Brussels Sprouts	Papaya (Non-GMO)
Cabbage	Red and Green Bell Peppers
Cantaloupe	Strawberries

There is also research out there about using laetrile/vitamin B17 for cancer treatment. Laetrile is effective at killing cancer cells and building the immune system to stop future outbreaks of cancer. You must have a very strict diet, which all cancer treatments should implement, along with several supplements. The main problem is that this knowledge is not being shared on a large scale. People have to do their own research to find out about it, and even then it is difficult to find a team of people to help you do these treatments properly. Because it is not mainstream, people are oblivious to it. Also, natural treatments for cancer are not covered by insurance companies so patients have to somehow find the funds necessary to try and get access to these treatments which can be costly, and for many people it is just not an option.

So this is great, right? We have two different natural treatments that are proven to be effective at killing and treating cancer cells! How come this isn't on the front page of every newspaper in the world? Well, the FDA strikes again. According to Cancer Tutor

> "The FDA has made the purchase of laetrile supplements effectively impossible, even though it is a perfectly natural and safe supplement. In order for a doctor to use laetrile supplements, they or their patient must 'confess' to the FDA that the doctor is using laetrile in their practice. In other words, laetrile supplements are effectively illegal because no doctor wants to admit they are using laetrile. Thus, if you illegally buy laetrile supplements, how do you insure you are buying it from a highly trusted source? This seems like an oxymoron. The FDA claims that laetrile is toxic. This is an absolute lie." [15]

Wouldn't it make sense to at least try to treat cancer with natural organic substances? No, that would be too easy and inexpensive. Is it at all bizarre to you that this may be the first time you have heard of these things? It is not an accident that you haven't. These companies have created toxic horrific poisons, inject them into people's bodies, tell them it is their only hope, and then laugh all the way to the bank while the patient dies and their family's lives are disrupted forever. Not to mention all the money that people donate to causes to help find a cure for cancer. All the wonderful organizations out there that have hundreds of volunteers who want to make a difference and save people's lives; and all their work is for naught, because the 'cure' we are all waiting for already exists. It has existed for decades. Corrupt corporations, and our government are keeping the cure for cancer hidden. Cancer is and always will be a business, unless we fight for change. I wonder everyday how these people sleep at night or look themselves in the mirror. What about all the children that die from cancer every year? According to the Environmental Protection Agency, cancer is the second leading cause of death among children ages 1-14, unintentional injuries being the leading cause. Although the causes of childhood cancer are not as well known, they state "Parental and childhood exposure to pesticides and radiation may cause certain cancers in children." [16]

According to Ron Gdanski, a health researcher, and the author of, **Cancer: *Cause, Cure and Cover-Up*** says in his article **"Childhood Cancer Epidemic"** that,

> "There is no proof that defective genes cause cancer. However, Dr Fibiger received the Nobel Prize in Medicine in 1926 for proving that parasitic larvae cause cancer. We now recognize that cancer starts with an injury to a mass of infected cells. Toxins and pollutants contribute to cancer by allowing infections to occur. Environmental pollutants such as residual DDT, lawn and garden sprays, household insect sprays and crop sprays can explain the rising incidence of infant cancer in rural areas. Chemical toxins disturb the cellular environment, which allows infectious parasitic life forms such as viruses, bacteria, fungi and parasite larvae to invade normal cells. Parasites provide the uncontrolled production of growth factors that cause warts, polyps, cysts, ulcers, lumps and other pre-cancerous lesions. Parasites also burrow into and weaken membrane barriers."[17]

He goes on to conclude that there are ways to protect and eliminate the formation of cancer cells from spreading in the body by cleansing the system of parasites, drinking fresh ozonated water, and eliminating meats and foods that have man-made chemicals in them.

Besides the fact that most children being treated for cancer in this country are not being exposed to the proper information about diet and nutrition during their treatments, there is also research that shows that children that are obese are more susceptible to cancers. So two of the biggest problems in our health epidemic, cancer and obesity, are not just main factors in adult health, but also in children. My main concern in this matter is that children do not have a choice. They are under the mercy of their parents, and doctors to make decisions for them. As parents we must become educated on these matters and we must make it our goal to then educate as many other parents as possible, so we can break the cycle! That is one of my goals in my lifetime. Research suggests that children with childhood obesity have a three times higher chance of getting cancer as children that do not have a serious medical condition such as obesity. I believe there are many natural ways we can protect our kids from these diseases daily with natural remedies we may even have sitting in our spice cabinet. Turmeric, for example is a powerful natural spice that has been shown to diminish cancer cell growth in animals. Of course the FDA hasn't approved it for any type of use for humans dealing with cancer but the information is starting to circulate through more western medically based organizations dealing with cancer. For example, according to an article published by the Mayo Clinic,

> "Curcumin, a substance found in the spice turmeric, has long been used in Asian medicine to treat a variety of maladies. Now some research suggests that curcumin may help prevent or treat cancer. Curcum-

in is thought to have antioxidant properties, which means it may decrease swelling and inflammation. It's being explored as a cancer treatment in part because inflammation appears to play a role in cancer. Laboratory and animal research suggests that curcumin may prevent cancer, slow the spread of cancer, make chemotherapy more effective and protect healthy cells from damage by radiation therapy. Curcumin is being studied for use in many types of cancer." [18]

Turmeric is a spice that you can readily get at the health food store. How much easier could it get to try and help your child get healthier, yet no traditional doctor will tell you this information. Doctors actually by law, cannot give out recommendations for natural therapies if you are undergoing cancer treatment. How corrupt is that? You hear about all sorts of clinical trials with cancer medications, but you never hear about clinical trials of cancer treatments using holistic remedies, and nutrition. Why? It is heartbreaking and disgusting to me to think that the people who are making these decisions on these medical health boards are not looking at all the options for treatments. Again, this goes back to the business side of things, which is beyond corrupt. It is criminal not to give people the right to know about these alternative methods, and to sit by the wayside and watch children and adults die of a disease that could be diminished, and cured in some cases, by following some simple steps of natural healing and good organic nutrition.

That is, in a nutshell, what is going on with the cancer business in our world. That is all it is, a business. I hate to break it to you people, but they don't want us to be healthy. I hope you are starting to see this. If we want health for our families and ourselves we will have to fight for it. We have to become educated, and we have to take matters in our own hands.

The greatest wealth is health. **- Virgil**

Vaccines- Silent Baby Killers?

In the last decade there has been a lot of talk about vaccines. Are they good, are they bad, are they necessary, are they worth the suggested risk? There are many tough and complicated questions when it comes to this controversial topic. Since the rise in infant and childhood vaccines amounts we have also see a rapid rise in the cases of autism and other neurological issues. Many argue, including the vaccine makers, CDC, and the government, that vaccines pose no risk and have no connection with autism or any other issues. Parents are under a tremendous amount of pressure from both the government and their Pediatricians to follow through with the suggested vaccine schedule without asking any questions or having any concern about the matter. Let's just say for a moment that I am neutral when it comes to this topic and let's just take a look at the cold hard facts. Since the 1980's when I was a young child until now the vaccine schedule has taken a giant leap from 10 vaccinations in 1983 to over 36 vaccinations in the first year of life in 2011.[19] According to the CDC, this drastic jump in scheduled vaccines is perfectly safe and posses no harm to young infants and children. However, when you take a closer look at the situation you find that the CDC has not done one study proving that increasing vaccines that drastically in the body of a tiny human with a newly functioning immune system is safe. During the same time period that the vaccine schedule was increased we are also seeing a rapid rise in cases of autism, ADHD, learning disabilities, and other neurological disorders in the same age group of the population that is being subjected to these shots. The CDC discusses this extreme rise on their website:

> "The Centers for Disease Control and Prevention (CDC) estimates that about 1 in 88 children has been identified with an autism spectrum disorder (ASD). This data comes from the Autism and Developmental Disabilities Monitoring (ADDM) Network, which estimated the number of 8-year-old children with ASDs living in 14 communities throughout the United States in 2008. This new estimate marks a 23% increase since our last report in 2009, and a 78% increase since our first report in 2007." [20]

Let's just use common sense for a minute. Since they know that there has been a constant increase in cases of autism, wouldn't it make sense to then look to any and all reasons why something would skyrocket so fast? Their argument for the rapid rise has to do with doctors and parents being that much more aware and thus being able to better diagnose. I am sorry but when something jumps 78% in a 2-year period that is a massive red flag to me. Not to mention there have been multiple situations in which vaccination even caused death in infants and young children. This is definitely not discussed in the mainstream media but it is happening. [21] Instead of the CDC and government agencies coming together with parents to do everything in their power to find the cause or research possible triggers, the conversation about the possible link between vaccines and these issues is rejected as false information. Because most parents' trust in their doctors and in these institutions, they are left with un answered questions and are bullied into making decisions that may not be right for their child.

In my own experience with the vaccine debacle I have had to argue, protect, and fight for my children's safety when it comes to the issue of the recommended vaccine schedule. For example, when I was having my first daughter Kayla I was adamant about not giving her the Hep B shot at the time of birth. Most parents don't even question this shot or the reason behind it, but it is a pointless shot for a newborn baby. The only way an infant can get Hep B is if the mother is already a carrier, and passed it to the baby in utero. A person would already know a head of time if they were positive for Hep B, as expectant mothers are tested for this early in pregnancy. At that point if the mother and child was inflicted the vaccine wouldn't matter anyway. The other way in which you contract the disease is through sexual activity or intravenous drug use. So as long as your baby isn't going to have sex or do some dope in the first several hours after they are born, it is safe to say they are not going to get Hep B. I had researched all of the vaccines, in detail, before I gave birth so I knew what my choice was on this matter. However, in California you have to request a written form in order to decline this shot, or it is automatically injected into your newborn baby. I actually had to argue with the nurse while I was in labor to please give me the form, as we were not going to allow this vaccine into our baby. It is just ridiculous that at such a precious time in life, you are forced to deal with these issues.

When I first started researching the vaccine debate it was a much more taboo topic than it is now. In the last several years, there has been many more parents and health professionals stepping forward to discuss their concerns about vaccine practices in the US. It is refreshing to see medical doctors start to question and speak out about this important matter. The International Medical Council on Vaccination is one such organization. Here is an overview of what they do according to their website:

"The International Medical Council on Vaccination is an association of medical doctors, registered nurses and other qualified medical professionals whose purpose is to counter the messages asserted by pharmaceutical companies, the government and medical agencies that vaccines are safe, effective and harmless. Our conclusions have been reached individually by each member of the Council, after thousands of hours of personal research, study and observation." [22]

- We are profoundly critical of the practice of vaccination. Vaccination is an unacceptable risk to every member of society, regardless of age.

- As medical professionals, Council members have observed first-hand the health of vaccinated vs. the unvaccinated.

- We find the latter group to be robust, healthy and drug-free compared to the former group.

- We have reviewed published studies in support of vaccines and have found them wanting in both substance and science.

- We have brought out into the open hundreds of peer-reviewed, published medical articles that document the damage and the diseases caused by vaccines.

- We find the premise of herd immunity to be a faulty theory.

- We encourage intelligent debate about vaccination.

- We expect individuals to take responsibility for their health and the health of their children by investigating the problems due to vaccination prior to subjecting their children, or themselves, to this medical procedure.

- We believe that refusing vaccination is a personal right that should be legislatively guaranteed.

My personal belief is that vaccines, just like other pharmaceuticals, pose a greater health risk than the issues they are trying to protect us against. With my first daughter I did one round of DTAP shots then decided to stop as the more I researched the scarier it got. We have not done any vaccinations with my youngest. I also recently had to switch Pediatricians to protect my right not to vaccinate my children. In our old office they had taken up a new practice, due to the pressure from the CDC and vaccine makers to push vaccines on parents, that they would actually make a parent declining a shot sign a waiver that basically said you were a bad parent and were putting your child in harms way by not choosing the shot. As soon as this started I was out of there! The 'safety testing' done for these vaccines is paid for and performed by the same companies that are producing the product. It is a major conflict of interest and I am not willing to let my children be science experiments. A great film to watch about the deceptive and controversial workings of the vaccine industry is, The Greater Good. I cried through this whole film because it is heartbreaking to see what other parents in the U. S. are going through. You can learn where to watch this film by looking at your **ECEG.** I am hoping at this point you are putting less faith and trust in these institutions and starting to ask some tough questions. The most important thing to know is that while this information may be scary and hard to take in, it is important we remember how powerful we are.

The Power Of Your Mind

I truly believe that the most important part of our human bodies is our minds. Our heart and our immune systems may be our biggest assets but without a healthy mind in control the body can become sick. Our minds control our thoughts, which control our beliefs, which control our actions, which control our results. I am a big believer in the power of thought to help our bodies' function with optimal health. If we believe that our bodies are sick and diseased, our bodies will become sick and diseased. If we believe in health and vitality, then that will be our reality. If we tell ourselves everyday that our bodies are the picture perfect example of health, even if they are not at that moment, we will start to put the forces in motion for this to become a reality. The power of your mind is more profound than any drug, any toxin, any disease, or aliment. I believe you can heal the body through intense focused thought. I also believe that 'the powers that be' know how phenomenal our minds can be, which is one reason why they work very hard to keep us distracted, sick, fearful, and focused on toxic thoughts. I believe the government is very afraid of us using our minds properly because at that point we may wake up and realize what is really happening to our health and our world. Using the power of the mind to heal the body is not a mainstream view and since I realize this is a hard concept for most people to grasp, I wanted to introduce you to my friend Nicholas Steele. Nicholas's story is one of the true power of the human spirit and mind. Truly we can heal from anything if we focus on it in the right way and his story exemplifies this power.

Nicholas was an amateur body builder when a freak accident left him paralyzed from the neck down. Although every doctor that worked on Nicholas told him he was going to die or be paralyzed for the rest of his life, Nicholas chose not to listen. Here is Nicholas's Story:

> "We all have an intrinsic mechanism to survive and achieve greatness. Sometimes we just lose our way. The best way to deal with any obstacle that life throws at us is to fight to win. Assess the situation, look for a solution, be positive in your outlook and visualize what you want. Really feel that you have achieved it. Keep reaffirming that you are a great person that you will succeed, that you will overcome all obstacles and visualize the perfect outcome. Keep saying and doing this day after day, night after night, even when

you're feeling low or on a high, the most important thing is to keep going and stay focused on only that which you want to achieve. When you do this and use the power of your own mind, you will beat any obstacle that life throws your way! The more positive energy that you have around you and in you enables you to fight and win. These are the exact principles I followed after my own accident.

In 2008 I broke my neck, crushing my spinal cord and destroying vertebrae C6 and C7. I was paralyzed from the neck down and told by doctors that I would remain this way for the rest of my life. I refused to accept their prognosis and told everyone that I would be home for Christmas. I made a promise to my little boy that I would be fine and he would get his 'big, strong dad' back soon.

Everyday, whilst I lay in bed, I visualized that I could walk, lift weights and play sports. I could see and feel each muscle and tendon working, pulling and pushing. I told myself over and over, 'I will walk again, I can do this, I am healing, I am a winner! Come on, Nicholas, you can do this! Get home for Christmas!' I did this day in and day out, until eventually the big toe on my right foot moved, then my right index finger, and slowly but surely over a number of months my limbs came back to life! My doctors were astounded. I was transferred to a rehabilitation unit where I continued to follow my visualization techniques and stay positive. The muscles in my legs were twitching and I could very weakly turn them in bed. I was making progress. So I kept working day in and day out, visualizing my body healing.

At this point even though there was progress, my arms refused to work. Then on a Monday morning, after an intense physical therapy session, I told my nurse I was going to stand up. With her help I leaned forward in my wheelchair, put my body's weight onto my legs and pushed with all my might. I slowly stood up and fell straight back down. I was ecstatic and my nurse cried. I stood several more times that day and by the end of the week I was walking unaided. From that point on, I knew I was going to make a full recovery. I did in fact, make it home for Christmas! My doctors called me a miracle. That was two years ago, and my story continues. I follow these principles everyday. I am grateful that I am alive and have great family and friends around me. Most importantly, I kept my promise to my son. If you truly want something in life you can achieve it. Never give up hope!"

Nicholas Steele

Nicholas is an inspiration to everyone he meets, and now you know why! When I met Nick his doctors and nutritionists had him on a 4,000-calorie a day diet to help him gain weight. Because of all his surgeries he was 100 lbs underweight! The doctors told him there was nothing they could do and he could now die from malnutrition. Nothing he tried worked. After a year of this regime, although Nick was making profound strides with his movement and healing, he had not put on one single pound. After meeting Nick, and learning of his incredible story, I knew I had to help him heal his body nutritionally. I introduced him to a nutrition and super food program called Isagenix. This program helped him put on an astonishing 12 pounds of lean muscle in less than nine weeks. He has gone on to put on 65 pounds of lean muscle in less than a year! We have become lifelong friends, and I admire everything about him and his courage not to give up. Just imagine if he had listened to what his doctors told him. Where would he be today? He would probably still be lying in a hospital bed paralyzed. I am grateful to God everyday for placing him in my life, and I know his story will impact so many lives. He is now a motivational speaker and is working on his first book. For more information on Isagenix and super foods, see Chapter 3 or view your **ECEG.**

"Science always has effects, but they are opposing effects - one that is destructive and one that is constructive. Science ruled by the intellect will splinter the view of the world into chaos of details, losing connection to the whole in the process. Science ruled by spirit, however, turns into wisdom, since it will be deeply moved by the wondrous overall scheme of things and feel respect and awe for the great mind felt to be at work behind it. Such is the difference between learnedness and wisdom."

Max Bircher-Benner, MD

Chapter 3

Good Nutrition Starts With Real Food

When it comes to eating right and exercising, there is no "I'll start tomorrow." Tomorrow is disease.

- Terri Guillemets

It is sad to say, but I am sure you have heard it many times already; we have become a fast food nation. Over the last fifty years our eating habits have become the worst in the world. We are officially the most overfed, yet undernourished country on the planet. We have been programmed by advertisements, media, and even movies about what things we should be eating and drinking. McDonalds has become a household name and worldwide phenomenon. There are over 33,000 McDonalds chains around the globe. This has become big business and has made many people multi, multi- millionaires. The problem is, it has come at a major cost, our health and well being. I am one of the few Americans that did not grow up on McDonalds or any other fast food for that matter. In fact, I can actually say I have never eaten at McDonalds in my life! It is not just McDonalds that is at fault, but it is the hundreds of other companies that are out there making processed, toxic food. The ingredients in fast food meals are actually not meant for the human body. They are filled with preservatives, additives, dyes, chemicals, and carcinogens. Carcinogens are chemical substances in the body that are cancer causing. I was at a fast food restaurant chain recently to use the restroom and they actually had a warning on the window about how the chemicals in the food they served could cause disease, yet there were at least a dozen people in their eating! That blew my mind. People don't even realize what they are doing to themselves on a daily basis. The phrase, 'you are what you eat' is taking on a whole new meaning in our toxic world. We are literally turning into ding-dongs, Big Macs, and corn. Our cells are so polluted with this junk that we are literally turning into junk.

There is a documentary called Processed People, which I highly recommend watching, that talks about this exact issue.

It is hard to get over the fact that someone or some corporation would deliberately put ingredients into foods that would actually cause the human body harm. Worse yet, that these products would actually cause the people that ate the food to become addicted to it. Well, unfortunately the world can be rough, as that is exactly what has happened. It comes down to one reason, greed. The food industry makes a lot of money off the products that they sell, and trust me, they are laughing all the way to the bank along with their pharmaceutical buddies. We have been programmed and taught to think that a burger, fries, and a coke are food. This meal is actually the #1 ordered meal in America. If we do not eat like this, than we are considered un-American. People have told me that I was un-American countless times over the years because I refused to eat these types of food. Billions of people eat fast food everyday. Some people eat fast food for all of their meals. If you have not seen the documentary Super Size Me, by Morgan Spurlock, I highly suggest you put this on your list of must see films. I will talk more about Morgan in a minute. Here are a few facts from his study: [23]

-Each day, 1 in 4 Americans visits a fast food restaurant

-In 1972, we spent 3 billion a year on fast food - today we spend more than $110 billion

-McDonald's feeds more than 46 million people a day - more than the entire population of Spain

-French fries are the most eaten vegetable in America

-You would have to walk for seven hours straight to burn off a Super Sized Coke, fry and Big Mac

-In the U.S., we eat more than 1,000,000 animals an hour

-80 percent of all Americans are either overweight or obese

-One in every three children born in the year 2000 will develop diabetes in their lifetime

-Left unabated, obesity will surpass smoking as the leading cause of preventable death in America

-Obesity has been linked to: Hypertension, Coronary Heart Disease, Adult Onset Diabetes, Stroke, Gall Bladder Disease, Osteoarthritis, Sleep Apnea, Respiratory Problems, Endometrial, Breast, Prostate and Colon Cancers, Dyslipidemia, steatohepatitis, insulin resistance, breathlessness, Asthma, Hyperuricaemia, reproductive hormone abnormalities, polycystic ovarian syndrome, impaired fertility and lower back pain

-The average child sees 10,000 TV advertisements per year

-Only seven items on McDonald's entire menu contain no sugar

-Willard Scott was the first Ronald McDonald - he was fired for being too fat

-McDonald's distributes more toys per year than Toys-R-Us

-Diabetes will cut 17-27 years off your life

-McDonald's: "Any processing our foods undergo make them more dangerous than unprocessed foods"

-The World Health Organization has declared obesity a global epidemic

-Eating fast food may be dangerous to your health

-McDonald's calls people who eat a lot of their food "heavy users"

-McDonald's operates more than 30,000 restaurants in more then 100 countries on 6 continents

-Before most children can speak they can recognize McDonald's

-Surgeon General David Satcher: "Fast food is a major contributor to the obesity epidemic"

-Most nutritionists recommend not eating fast food more than once a month

-40 percent of American meals are eaten outside the home

-McDonald's represents 43% of total U. S. fast food market

"We think fast food is equivalent to pornography, nutritionally speaking."
Steve Elbert

It is not a new fact that obesity is at an all time high. We are literally eating ourselves to death! 85 percent of Americans are overweight, and 35 percent meet the criteria for obesity. The saddest statics to me of all is that an estimated 30 million children are obese. That, my friend, is not ok. Children are getting diagnosed with type 2 Diabetes at ages 4 and 5. Type 2 Diabetes is a lifestyle disease, it is from the foods you eat, and how you take care of your body. The saddest part is, these kids do not have a choice. They have to eat whatever is put in front of them, so if Mom and Dad go through the drive through every day to get their fried processed foods, that is what the kids will get too. Do you think that Ronald McDonald was a marketing mistake? More like marketing genius. How do you get adults to buy more of something? Have their kids want to have it too. It is ironic to me that a lot of fast food companies donate to charities that deal with childhood diseases like cancer and leukemia, when actually their foods and the toxic ingredients they use are playing a huge part in the degeneration of health and the onset of things like cancer. Maybe that is how they can sleep at night. At least they are pretending like they care.

We provide food that customers love, day after day after day. People just want more of it.
Ray Kroc Owner and Founder of McDonald's

More than 60 percent of American adults and 13 percent of children and adolescents are classified as overweight or obese. The adult figure has doubled since 1980; for children and adolescents it has tripled. In 2000, the U. S. healthcare system spent $61 billion on the diagnosis, care, and prevention of obesity. Last year alone, Americans spent about $115 billion on fast food. That is more than what was spent on higher education, personal computers, or new cars combined. Americans spend about half of their food budget on meals and drinks consumed outside the home, and consume about a third of their daily energy this way. Do any of these statistics seem normal to you?

When Food Was Food

The other day I was shopping at Whole Foods. I remember the days when Whole Foods was a little health food store that started in California called Mrs. Gouches. This was the only store my mother shopped at growing up, so I spent a lot of time there. I have some very fond memories of going to get our organic groceries at Mrs. Gouches. I was raised in a very health conscious household. My Mom was a vegetarian and my Dad ate meat. My brother and I had the choice of whether we wanted to eat meat or not. It was not forced on us, but ironically enough both of us decided at a very young age that we wanted to be vegetarian. I remember being about three years old sitting at the dinner table, and my Mom had made ribs for my Dad. My brother, who was seven years old at the time, was obsessed with Dinosaurs. Out of the blue, he took his rib that he was eating, threw it down on the plate and exclaimed, "I feel like Tyrannosaurus Rex, and I never want to eat meat again!" I don't remember if I was even eating the ribs or not, but, I vividly remember making a pact with my brother in the bathroom that night that we did not want to eat meat anymore. I have been a vegetarian ever since. It is funny the things we remember about childhood, but that actually became a pretty pivotal moment in my life. So, back to my memories at Mrs. Gouches. This store was nothing like the Whole Foods now. Everything, and I do mean everything was 100 percent natural. They did not carry anything with white flour or refined sugar. I find myself having to check labels at Whole Foods now to ensure that things are really "all natural" and checking to see what kind of sweeteners are being used. With the GMO (genetically modified organism) scandal happening right now, I am putting less faith in what Whole Foods has to offer. I still shop there from time to time to get certain things, and they do stock some amazing products, but as soon as it became a big corporation, the game changed forever. Plus with the pressures of the major food industry monopolies wanting to put GMOs on shelves everywhere, I believe Whole Foods has really caved in.

GMOs -The Battle for Our Lives

A few months ago in my home state of California, there was a proposition put on the ballot that would require companies to label GMO ingredients in their products. Prop 37, as it was called, was the first big political step from the grassroots movement of organic consumers to take the stage nationally about the important issue of GMOs. Before Prop 37 many people were not even aware of what a GMO was! Due to Prop 37 and the impressive work of the Non-GMO movement, people became more aware then ever before what was happening behind the veil of the food industry. Even though it was a state election it became a national conversation. Even some celebrities got on board and made funny and informative YouTube videos to educate the public about GMOs and their deadly effects. Unfortunately, do to the massive amounts of advertising and money that was pumped into stopping Prop 37 from the Big Agro corporations, such as Monsanto and DuPont, the public was once again fooled and the prop didn't pass. Today the U. S. is one of the only industrialized nations in the world that does not require GMO labeling laws. Sixty- four other countries have instituted both tough regulations and labeling, or outlawed GMO products and seeds all together. [24] I guess in America, the supposed greatest Democracy in the world, we don't get the right to know what we are eating.

This is the sorry state of our food industry right now. Large corporations have taken over the food industry and control every aspect. GMOs are the only product in history to create successful multi-million dollar revenues by completely lying to the consumer base that is buying the product. Again, if the government cared about our health they would never let something like this happen. The major food corporations have huge lobbying power in Washington. The top selling GMO products that you most likely consume on a daily basis are corn, canola, soy, wheat, and sugar. It is clear that Monsanto and their cohorts are not going anyway with out a major fight. Believe it or not only a few large companies produce most of the foods we consume. The top companies that are on my crap list are General Mills, Foster Farms, Kellogg's, Coca Cola, Pepsi, and the worst one is Monsanto. They are all connected in some aspect financially and the same core, group of people run the biggest companies in America. If you follow the money trail it leads into the secret societies that control and run, not only our food systems, but also our banking systems, and our government. It is a scandalous lie that has most of the world fooled. I am not going to go into detail about these secret societies but you should be aware that they absolutely exist and they are not out there to protect us. To learn more about the inner workings of these groups watch the film Thrive. Evil has indeed seeped into every aspect of our so-called freedoms. To learn more about GMOs and what you can do to protect yourself visit your **ECEG**.

If you have not seen these documentaries and you care about your health in the slightest, I suggest you go out tonight and rent them all!

-Food Inc

-Food Matters

-King Corn

-Super Size Me

-Thrive

-Genetic Roulette

-The Greater Good

These films depict the graphic nature of the state of our food and country for that matter. This will educate you about how it is being produced, the nutrition, or lack there of, and the greed and corruption in this industry. The information in these films will astound you. I know I was in shock for sometime after really absorbing all of this information. Just take it one step at a time and congratulate yourself for being open to learning the truth.

> "We put faith in our government to protect us, and we're not being protected at the most basic level."
> -- Barbara Kowalcyk, a heroic mother whose 2 1/2 year old child Kevin died from E. coli. She has since become a food safety advocate, fighting to give the USDA back its power to shut down plants that repeatedly produce contaminated meats. (Barbara and her

mother, Patricia Buck, have pushed for the "Kevin's Law" bill to become law since 2002. It still has not passed.)

The Toxic Food Industry

Here is the awful truth about our foods right here, right now in this country. On average we have 65-70 insecticides, pesticides, and herbicides sprayed on our fruits and vegetables. Even if you eat organically you are still exposed to a lot of these chemicals. Though organic is always the better option, there is still cross contaminations happening. Meat, cheese, and milk are filled with hormones, steroids, antibiotics, and bacteria. I will talk more about milk in a minute. Our grains are processed, bleached, and mechanically produced. Most of the foods we eat are frozen, which kills all the live nutrition, then they are micro waved which fills it with deadly cancerous waves, then we splatter it with high fat dressings, sauces, and refined salts that add even more chemicals and toxins to the body. This is what is happening to our good "fresh foods". As we talked about earlier, fast food is filled with preservatives, dyes, chemicals, additives, carcinogens, fillers, plastics, and many other harmful impurities. Recent information has even surfaced that certain popular fast food chains use horsemeat in their products. To say that we have truly turned into a fast food nation would be an understatement. The nasty truth about fast food is, it is not really food! It is actually not meant for the human body! If you think I am joking just watch the documentaries that I mentioned earlier and you will get a better grasp on the big picture. For example, in the film Super Size Me, Morgan Spurlock starts off completely healthy and decides to experiment with eating McDonald's for thirty days for all three meals a day. By the end of the thirty-day period Morgan became extremely sick, had gained a tremendous amount of weight, and his doctor actually told him to stop the experiment because he was risking his health. Wait a second, why would someone get sick from eating at a restaurant that is supposed to be providing people with food for their bodies? Because, again, fast food, is literally not real food! If you ate real food for thirty days consisting of non-gmo vegetables, fruits, and whole grains, you would not be putting your body in jeopardy or risking your life, would you? But when you eat fast food, especially if you eat it on a regular basis, you are literally risking your life. If you give it to your children, you are one step away from child abuse in my opinion. I believe that one day, it will be considered child abuse to feed your children toxic chemicals that are so damaging to their health.

As parents, it is our responsibility to provide our children with the proper nutrition, ensure their safety, and provide them with the best quality of life. Taking them to fast food chains is not doing any of those things. There is now research coming out showing that the wrappers and receipts from fast food restaurants even contain the toxic chemical BPA. BPA was the chemical that was removed from baby bottles and children's sippy cups a few years ago because of its link to cancer and other diseases. Now, not only is your fast food extremely toxic, but what they package it in is a deadly material as well. I know this may all be a little overwhelming, but it is the truth. Toxic ingredients make toxic food, wrapped in toxic containers, produce toxic people! It is so simple, yet so few people choose to be aware of these factors.

I have had numerous people say to me that they can't eat certain natural foods, or do certain health programs because they have "allergies" yet they will be sitting there drinking a diet coke, and just ate fast food for lunch. Well, I hate to break it to you, but the fast food and the soda are a big reason for your body not functioning properly, which can lead to allergies, imbalances, and of course disease. The other part of the food debacle that most people don't understand is how food affects the brain. When you eat junk food it literally alters your brain chemistry, just like when you eat healthy foods the same happens, but for the positive. Certain ingredients like, high fructose corn syrup (HFCS), which is in almost all junk and processed foods, is extremely toxic to the body and the brain. There are many reasons why I hate this product. Yes, I used the word hate, because I really think it is an evil thing. HFCS mess with the neurotransmitters in your brain that tell you that you are full. Therefore, when you consume a lot of foods with this ingredient in it you tend to overeat, or feel constantly hungry. This is another reason obesity is on the rise. Secondly, there has been research indicating that when they make HFCS they actually use Mercury to process it. That means every time you ingest it, you are taking in small amounts of Mercury. Mercury causes a whole range of problems in the body, and has been linked to such diseases as Alzheimer's, and Lou Gehrig's disease. Thirdly, HFCS come from corn and about 88%-90% of all corn in the U. S. is genetically modified, and I promise you that they are not using organic corn to produce HFCS. When I coach people I always tell my clients to get this ingredient out of their homes as soon as possible. It is deadly and should be taken off the market. HFCS is found in the following products

- **-Regular Sodas**
- **-Breakfast Cereal**
- **-Yogurt**
- **-Bread, even whole wheat bread (check the back)**
- **-Ketchup**
- **-Cookies**
- **-Many snack foods**

-Candy

-Pastries

-And many, many other products that you may consume on a daily basis

The other ingredient that I hate is aspartame. Aspartame came on the scene to "reduce the sugar intake" in certain sodas, and other products. These products started to be marketed as "diet foods" and "weight loss foods". This is also a product that is recommended for people with diabetes, since diabetics have to watch their sugar intake. Aspartame is one of the deadliest ingredients out there, in my opinion. It is a known carcinogen, remember that means it can cause cancer, and it affects many of your body's normal functions, including hormones, reproductive organs, and brain function. When Aspartame is tested on rats in laboratories they usually die from some sort of cancerous tumor. Aspartame alone has been linked to over 90 various health issues including depression and even suicide! According to Medical News Today, studies were done by the Environmental Health Perspectives Organization (EHP). The authors of the study were the first to demonstrate that aspartame had multiple carcinogenic effects when administered to rats in feed. They called for an "urgent reevaluation" of the current guidelines for the use and consumption of this product. Apparently their cry was not heard.

> "Our study has shown that aspartame is a multipotential carcinogenic compound whose carcinogenic effects are also evident at a daily dose of 20 milligrams per kilogram of body weight (mg/kg), notably less than the current acceptable daily intake for humans," the authors write. Currently, the acceptable daily intake for humans is set at 50 mg/kg in the United States and 40 mg/kg in Europe.
> Aspartame is the second most widely used artifi-

cial sweetener in the world. It is found in more than 6,000 products including carbonated and powdered soft drinks, hot chocolate, chewing gum, candy, desserts, yogurt, and tabletop sweeteners, as well as some pharmaceutical products like vitamins and sugar-free cough drops. More than 200 million people worldwide consume it. The sweetener has been used for more than 30 years, having first been approved by the FDA in 1974. Studies of the carcinogenicity of aspartame performed by its producers have been negative." [25]

Interesting that the studies done by the companies that are producing this product didn't showcase its carcinogenic effects. It is infuriating to me that this corruption can go on. I am sorry, but why is this product allowed to be anywhere near our foods or beverages! It is a poison and should be taken off the market immediately. The answer as to why this hasn't happen again is greed and power. It is not an accident that these companies make products like this. It is all part of a plan to make you sicker, fatter, and stupider, literally. If you don't believe me, do your research and see the companies that supply these products. They are all linked back to the major companies that control the entire industrial food industry and influence our government. There is one major corporation that is really at the root of it all. For the sake of my families' safety, and mine, we will just call this situation, ***The Silent Scandal***, and what a scandal it is! This major corporation is responsible for the majority of the poison going into our foods. I am sure if you do your research you can figure out which specific company I am talking about.

The Silent Scandal

There is a huge corporation that supplies, manufactures, and subsidies the chemicals sprayed on our foods. They control the farm and dairy industry, and they also have links to the pharmaceutical industry. The documentary Food Inc, graphically shows what is really going on with our farm industry, and how much control this scandal really has over all of us. Because of this company and their ties with the government many small farms have been shut down, or bullied into treating their animals poorly, injecting them with chemicals, and getting rid of all their organic seeds. This company holds patents on all of these GMO seeds, so they run a monopoly of the food supply. Most of our corn, soybeans, wheat, canola, and even certain vegetables and fruits are grown from GMO seeds. There are many government officials that are linked to this scandal, which is why this company can get away with what they are doing. A Supreme Court justice was an attorney at this company from 1976 to 1979. After his appointment to the Supreme Court, he wrote the majority opinion in a case that helped them enforce their seed patents. They have people working on the inside for them, to ensure that their toxic deadly products get approved, and have no legal consequences. It is a silent scandal that is literally killing America!

In Food Inc, it shows the farmers that have tried to fight against them and have miserably lost due to lack of power and money. One gentleman refused to show his face on camera because he was scared for his life, and had been threatened by them. He had workers from this company following him and harassing him. You can see now why I also want to be careful of what I say. What kind of Democracy do we live in where a company can get away with acting like this?

Here is what this company says on their website as their mission statement.

>Billions of people depend upon what farmers do. And so will billions more. In the next few decades, farmers will have to grow as much food as they have in

> the past 10,000 years – combined.
> It is our purpose to work alongside farmers to do exactly that.
> To produce more food.
> To produce more with less, conserving resources like soil and water.
> And to improve lives.
> We do this by selling seeds, traits developed through biotechnology, and crop protection chemicals.

I love the 'Improve Lives' line. What a wonderful impact they are making in the world, not! It is clear that they do not really care about farmers and improving lives. If they did care about farmers and the people, why have they completely monopolized the industry, shut down hundreds of family run farms and continue to poison and manipulate our food? Here are just a few quotes from people that are in the thick of it with this company.

> They have, " a team of private investigators that kinda roam the country and they have a little 1-800 hotline ... if you save your own seed, you're gonna get a call." -Troy Roush, VP, American Corn Growers Association, on what's happening behind the scenes to America's farmers.
> "I found it necessary to get up at 3 or 4 in the morning before the (private) investigators are on the road following me." - Moe Parr, an Indiana man who was sued by this company for inducing farmers to violate patents by seed cleaning – a practice utilized by farmers for thousands of years. Parr, who has been a seed cleaner for 25 years, was subsequently pushed out of the seed business.

This scandal is a business powerhouse. Or, should I say, a business slaughterhouse. In 2008 they made over $2 billion in net profits and $11 billion in revenues. They are expected to reach similar numbers for the coming years, if not more. Not to shabby for a company that is getting away with murder, literally.

According to Dr Mercola, a well-respected natural health advocate, this company is one of the "greatest risks to your health". He went on to name a few reasons why this company is so deadly to our health.

> Why is Monsanto top on my hit list of evil corporations? Here is just a short list of the many improprieties and outright crimes committed by Monsanto:
> - Suing small farmers for patent infringement after Monsanto's GM seeds spread wildly into surrounding farmers' fields, contaminating their conventional crops
> -Secretly discharging PCB-laden toxic waste into an Alabama creek, and dumping millions of pounds of PCBs into open-pit landfills for decades after PCBs were banned in the U. S. for being a possible carcinogen.
> -Being found guilty of bribery to bypass Indonesian law requiring an environmental assessment review for its genetically engineered cotton.
> -Last year, the supreme court of France found Monsanto guilty of falsely advertising its herbicide Roundup as "biodegradable" and "environmentally friendly." Scientific evaluation discovered that glyphosate, the active ingredient in RoundUp, is acutely toxic to fish and birds and can kill beneficial insects and soil organisms that maintain ecological balance. Additionally, the surfactant ingredient in Roundup is more acutely toxic than glyphosate itself, and the combination of the two is even more toxic.
> In 2007, the South African Advertising Standards Authority also found Monsanto guilty of lying when advertising, "no negative reactions to Genetically Modified food have been reported."
> -According to one EPA scientist, Monsanto doctored studies and covered-up dioxin contamination of a wide range of its products. She concluded that the company's behavior constituted "a long pattern of fraud."
> -In 1999, the New York Times exposed that Monsanto's PR firm, Burson Marsteller, had paid fake "pro-GMO" food demonstrators to counteract a group of

> anti-biotech protesters outside a Washington, DC FDA meeting.
> This should give you a clue as to why I'm thrilled that Monsanto appears to be falling out of favor, at least in the stock market realm. [26]

He also goes on to state that this scandal has lots of help on the "inside" to ensure that their toxic products and power over Americans remains intact.

> "And they've got help at every turn, including from leaders in the U. S. government. Michael Taylor, a former vice president of public policy and chief lobbyist at Monsanto Company, is the deputy commissioner for foods at the U. S. Food and Drug Administration (FDA).
> Who is Michael Taylor? He is the person who "oversaw the creation of GMO policy," according to Jeffrey Smith, the leading spokesperson on the dangers of GM foods. Smith continues:
> "If GMOs are indeed responsible for massive sickness and death, then the individual who oversaw the FDA policy that facilitated their introduction holds a uniquely infamous role in human history. That person is Michael Taylor. He had been Monsanto's attorney before becoming policy chief at the FDA. Soon after, he became Monsanto's vice president and chief lobbyist."
> The FDA policy being referred to is the 1992 GMO policy, which stated:
> "The agency is not aware of any information showing that foods derived by these new methods [genetic engineering] differ from other foods in any meaningful or uniform way."
> In reality, there was major concern among FDA scientists that GM foods were in fact different than natural foods, and that their creation could prompt unknown and unpredictable health problems.
> Former Iowa Governor Tom Vilsack, now the Secretary of Agriculture, is also widely regarded as a shill for biotech giants like Monsanto (he even reportedly

often travels in Monsanto's jet). There are other less noticeable connections too, such as Sharon Long, a former member of Monsanto's board of directors who was part of Obama's scientific advisory team during the election/campaign." (26)

It is hard to fight against the man, but we have to. Even as I am writing this book, there are things and facts I would like to say, but I also want to protect my family and myself. Wow, what a democracy we live in! How did we fall victim to such a disastrous situation. If people only knew how much power they have, we could make so many positive changes and stop this monarchic situation from going on. I believe it is a cause worth fighting for. After all, if you don't have your health, what do you have?

Super Foods-Where Real Nutrition Begins

Now that we have discussed some of the dangers of regular food, fast food, and some of the evils that exist in the food industry, let us turn it to a more positive light. Let us talk about the most important thing for your health, good nutrition. Good nutrition, starts with real food! Super foods are, in my opinion, the best way to ensure proper health and nutrition, considering our dire situation of nutritionally bankrupt and toxic foods. Super foods are foods that give the body a power packed punch of the essential nutrients we need in a condensed form. I have been an advocate of super foods for many years, and I am always fascinated by the plethora of information out there and the current research that is coming forward about them. Yet, even in a progressive state like California it is astounding to me how many people do not utilize the health benefits of super foods regularly. I was at a party recently and was discussing health with a gentleman that was there, and he actually said to me, "What are super foods, I have never heard of that." I was shocked. When I asked him what he had eaten for lunch, he replied, "McDonalds." I believe that if people knew how easy it is to be healthy, they would be.

Super foods have been used by various cultures all over the world for millions of years. Some of the healthiest cultures on the planet owe their good health to the nutritional benefits of the super foods that they eat. The Mayans swore by raw cacao, and this super food is rapidly becoming one of the most loved super foods on the market right now. Cacao was very special and sacred to the Mayans, and it was even used as a form of currency by them and Aztec civilizations. Cacao is the main ingredient in all forms of real chocolate. It is one of the primary sources of magnesium from nature and is jam packed with antioxidants. It is also a mood enhancer, due to the abundant presence of neurotransmitters, such as phenyl ethylamine (PEA), anandamide (the bliss chemical), dopamine and serotonin (anti-depressants) in raw cacao. Dark chocolate is very effective in helping to treat pain and manage mental imbalances. I personally consume a lot of raw cacao along with another super food chocolates called Isa Delight. Isa Delights are organic Belgium dark chocolates that are packed with amino acids, vitamins, minerals, and green tea. They help to lift your mood, decrease cravings, and help with pain, weight loss, stress reduction, and energy. They are fabulous and I eat them everyday! For more information about eating raw cacao and Isa Delights please go to www.besttotalbodycleanse.com.

Another wonderful super food is Spirulina. Spirulina is a type of blue-green algae. It is a native component of South American and African alkaline lakes. Spirulina is an essential component of our Earth that actually helped to produce all the oxygen in the atmosphere as the Earth was being formed. They were actually the first form of pytosynthetic life and it is more than thirty-five billion years old! This amazing food is considered a "whole food" because of its complete nutritional profile. It is one of the best sources of vegetarian proteins on the planet. My daughters and I have a scoop of green super foods, which contains spirulina, in our morning shake everyday to ensure we are getting the proper amount of greens in our system. There are dozens of super foods that do extraordinary stuff to the human body. I always say that if you want to be a super human, eat super foods, it is that easy. Real foods have nutrition in them, they come from the earth, and they have been around for centuries. Fake foods or processed foods have no nutrition in them, they come from chemicals and factories, and they have been around for less than sixty years. Which do you think you should put in your body?

My friend, Dr. Tony O'Donnell, whom I mentioned earlier, formulates the greens I use. Dr. O'Donnell is a genius when it comes to formulations and is known as the Herb Doc. When he partnered with John Anderson and Isagenix the world was given a double blessing. I will talk more about John in a minute. Each ingredient is hand selected by Dr. O'Donnell and is from the highest quality sources in the world. Earlier we talked about several companies that are doing really awful things to our health and the planet. I would now like to talk about some people and companies that are making a huge positive impact in the world, and who are fighting against all the issues we have been discussing.

Isagenix

I personally use a system that has the highest quality organic super foods on the planet, called Isagenix. Isagenix is a super food system designed to help your body start functioning properly again. The formulator, John Anderson, is a nutrition genius. After thirty-five years in the nutrition field being one of the top nutritional formulators in the world, John retired a very wealth man. He is an avid world traveler and he had always searched the globe to find the highest quality nutrients. The problem was that the companies he worked for didn't always give him the creative rights to make the kind of high quality products he wanted to. John said, "No one ever let me make the kind of nutritional products that I wanted to." After being bitten by a Brown Recluse spider, Johns own health was in dire shape. Through his experience and knowledge of cleansing and super foods John was able to help his body heal and rejuvenate again. John came out of retirement in 2002, and decided to combine all his years of knowledge and expertise to create the world's most perfect food. He partnered with a highly successful couple, Jim and Kathy Coover. Jim and Kathy had over twenty-five years of experience in the direct sales and network marketing industry. They were also independently wealthy and had just retired when John approached them. After trying John's new products they knew they had something that could really change the world. It was then that Isagenix was born. Their mission is:

> "To impact world health and to free people from both physical and financial pain, and in the process create the largest health and wellness company in the world."

Isagenix is truly staying true to their mission of impacting lives. Since 2002 over 300,000 people worldwide have been blessed with these products. They have helped hundreds of people lose hundreds of pounds, and have helped thousands of people regain their health, energy, and vitality. The Isagenix system is comprised of over 252 organic compounds, over seventy organic trace minerals, live active enzymes, vitamins, essential amino acids, fatty acids, electrolytes, and many other components that the body needs. I personally owe my own health to John and his creation. They are one of the few companies that do what they say, and they make "no compromise" products.

I was introduced to these amazing products and company when I was 2 months pregnant with my first child, my daughter Kayla. I was having some health challenges and was not feeling well. Because I am a vegetarian, getting enough protein and iron had always been a challenge for me. I had also dealt with some blood sugar imbalances for most of my childhood, and adult life. When I got pregnant all of these issues magnified. During my first month of pregnancy I was having fainting spells, and was not feeling well at all. When my doctor did my first round of blood work it was not very good in certain areas. My protein levels where low, my blood sugar was imbalanced, and my iron levels were dangerously low. My doctor looked at me and said, "Well, you have to start eating red meat", as if that was my only option to get my body balanced. I obviously didn't take her advice, and I started to look for other options to increase my protein and iron. Mind you, at the time I had an all-organic diet, I was eating a perfectly balanced amount of vegetarian proteins, and I ate consistently to keep my blood sugars balanced, yet I was still having problems! This stemmed from the fact that my body was not absorbing the nutrition I was eating. Plus, the organic foods I was consuming were still not nutritionally complete, due to the factors we have been discussing. I actually remember praying to God to give me some sort of answer so that I could have the proper health and nutrition during my pregnancy. I knew that I wanted to have an all-natural birth, and I wanted to ensure optimal health for my child each step of the way. The same week I got my blood work back, my cousin Erin called me up and told me about an amazing experience she had been having with some products called Isagenix. She told me this system had literally changed her life in a few days. I immediately went to see her and was happily surprised at how vibrant and healthy she looked. Erin had gone through her own health challenges over the previous years and had completely burned herself out. The last time I had seen her she looked exhausted and sick, because she was. This time she looked vibrant and healthy! She told my Mom and I about this product, and what it had done for her health in just a few days. My mom and I are very open to nutrition, obviously, so we decided to give it a try as well. I looked at all the ingredients in their meal replacement shake and was blown away by all the nutrition it had in it. I was already doing a shake for breakfast, which was apparently doing nothing for me as far as my health and protein levels, so I decided to give Isagenix a try.

On day four of doing only one shake for breakfast, I felt better than I had ever felt in my entire life, even before I was pregnant! My energy was amazing, my mind was clear, my morning sickness had subsided, and my body felt at ease. I didn't' know what had happened until three weeks later when the doctor tested my blood again. She walked in, looked at me and said, "Wow, you must have started eating a lot of steak!" I said no, and asked why. She said "because your blood work is perfect. Your iron and protein levels are perfect, and your blood sugar is completely balanced!" I explained to her that I had not eaten any red meat and that I was just doing an organic shake for breakfast. She was shocked that my levels had improved that much, and that red meat had not been apart of it. She told me to keep doing whatever I was doing because something was working very well. I have put Isagenix in my body everyday since. The program also helped me to release my baby weight in two weeks after having Kayla. Kayla has also been on Isagenix since she started solid foods as a baby and I recently started my youngest on them as well. My Mom went on the lose her post menopausal weight of thirty plus pounds in less than six weeks, and went from an exhausted size ten to an energetic size two! Needless to say, it had a profound effect on our lives.

Since that day I have helped thousands of people through the program. It is one of my passions to share this gift with others, because that is what Isagenix is, a true gift! It is by far the best nutrition on the planet and my family will always eat Isagenix super foods for the rest of our lives. Whether you are looking to lose weight, properly cleanse your body, get the adequate amount of nutrition, have more energy, or even sleep better, Isagenix can help. I will go over nutritional cleansing in more detail in the detoxify chapter. For more information go to www.besttotalbodycleanse.com or your **ECEG**.

Minerals

So what were the most important things missing from the organic foods that I was eating, and why was it so hard for me to absorb the nutrition? The answer has to do with minerals. Minerals are the most important aspect of foods for the body. Your body needs over sixty minerals to function properly everyday. Most minerals we need should be found in our foods, but sadly they are not anymore. Remember all the death we talked about earlier that is sprayed all over our food? Well, the worst part about that death, other than the fact that it is really gross they spray poison on our foods, is that when the chemicals go on to the fruit or vegetable they also leak down into the topsoil. The topsoil is extremely important for helping the plant get nutrition. This death not only kills the insects that were eating the crops, it also kills the microorganisms that live in the top soil that help convert the rock mineral into something that can be absorbed and obtained by the plant. Since these organisms have been killed off, the minerals and nutrients cannot get up into our foods. Farmers know this, and that is why organic farmers do not use these toxic chemicals. The large farming corporations do not take the time to allow the soil to rest and rejuvenate and they only put a fraction of the minerals needed back in the soil. Out of the 70 that should be present, only 3 usually make it back in. Those minerals are nitrogen, potassium, and phosphorus. All the rest are missing! If they are missing from our foods, that means they are missing from our bodies. Minerals are like the spark plugs of life; you need them to live. That was what was missing from my body that Isagenix helped me put back in.

John Anderson was known as the "Mineral Man" in the nutrition industry. He is an expert at finding the best sources of organic trace minerals and putting them back into the body. Thank you John! The missing link to health lies in the missing minerals. I received this email from a friend of mine, Dave MacArthur, the other day. Dave is a wonderful man who is also very passionate about educating people about these topics. We like to say that we are on a 'Health Crusade'. Dave is a phenomenal cleansing coach, speaker, and entrepreneur. He has helped thousands of people change their lives through proper nutrition and education. Here is what Dave's email said:

Did you know according to recent studies over **90%** of what people eat is processed? Take a look at this:

-Many people think that FOOD is something you eat to get pleasure or to reward & treat yourself with. There actually is no definition of food in that regard (that is something that irresponsible advertising has portrayed)

-The actual definition of FOOD: That which is eaten to sustain life, provide energy, and promote the growth and repair of tissue; in other words, NOURISHMENT.

-According to this definition then people are eating something other than food

-The essential nutrients in FOOD required to sustain life are:

1. Amino Acids

2. Fatty Acids

3. Vitamins

4. Minerals

5. Enzymes

- 90% of the "FOOD" people are eating (processed) is either missing these all together or do not have the adequate amounts

-DIET: 1). A regulated course of FOOD & drink to promote health 2). To eat according to prescribed rules

-DIET stems from a word meaning "a way of living" which is *a big contrast* from today's meaning of diet of calorie depravation and depriving

We can learn a lot right there from that short, but sweet, overview of diet and nutrition. We have been grossly misinformed about what "food" really is. Most real foods are not even consumed by the average American on a daily basis. Instead we stuff our faces with fake foods that are literally doing us more harm than good. We need to get back to nature, and we need to get back to eating real foods.

Organic Vs. Non-Organic

Because the organic craze has become popular many people are starting to believe that "organics" are just a fad term and a marketing ploy. This is not the case. Organic foods under go much stricter regulations than conventionally farmed foods. While it is almost impossible to eat 100% organic all the time, you can make a substantial effort in reducing the number of pesticides, and other chemicals on your foods by purchasing organically grown and locally grown fruits and vegetables. People also tend to think that eating organically is much more expensive. While certain markets due up -charge on organic foods, you can find many reasonably priced and affordable organic foods at your local markets. Even Wal-Mart is starting to carry more and more organic choices. Recently I was back in Wisconsin visiting family and wanted to make a trip to the store to buy some organic groceries. My aunt and cousin told me that there weren't really any health food stores around, and they didn't know where I could get any 'weird' California organic foods. Wal-Mart was my only option. So, my Mom and I set out to Wal-Mart, determined to find some healthy choices for our stay. I was presently surprised to find quite a selection of organic products at the store. Although it was not my optimal selection, we were able to purchase about 85 percent of our products organically. All we had to do was look. That is one of the problems, people are not educated about healthier choices so they literally do not see or look for them when they are shopping. They just pick up the brands, and items they see in commercials and advertisements without even thinking about the ingredients that are in them. I personally shop at Trader Joe's, Sprouts Market, my Isagenix online store, and the local farmers markets. I actually went into Albertson's the other day and was disgusted at the lack of organic choices in the store. There was a tiny section of overpriced organic vegetables that did not even look that fresh, and the organic fruit selection was non-existent. I literally could not find anything that I wanted to purchase in that store. I was walking up and down the isles looking at all the shelves filled with non-food, food items. It was heartbreaking to say the least. It is so unjust and unfair to not even give people a chance to try and be healthy.

"Every day I wake up looking for a way to convey one of the most important messages of our time: if you want to change the world, change how you eat."
Dave Murphy Founder and Executive Director Food Democracy Now!

Lets take a look at organic vs. non-organic fruits and vegetables. A popular study called, The Dirty Dozen, was released showcasing the twelve most toxic fruits and vegetables on the market. Here is what made the list: [27]

    Most Contaminated
    -Peaches
    -Apples
    -Sweet Bell Peppers
    -Celery
    -Nectarines
    -Strawberries
    -Cherries
    -Pears
    -Grapes (Imported)
    -Spinach
    -Lettuce
    -Potatoes
    Least Contaminated
    -Onions
    -Avocado
    -Sweet Corn (Frozen)
    -Pineapples
    -Mango
    -Asparagus
    -Sweet Peas (Frozen)
    -Kiwi Fruit
    -Bananas
    -Cabbage
    -Broccoli
    -Papaya

According to an article by Dr. Mercola,

> " The Environmental Protection Agency (EPA) considers 60 percent of herbicides, 90 percent of fungicides, and 30 percent of insecticides to be carcinogenic, and most are damaging to your nervous system as well. In fact, these powerful and dangerous chemicals have been linked to numerous health problems such as:
> -Neurotoxicity
> -Disruption of your endocrine system
> -Carcinogenicity
> -Immune system suppression
> -Male infertility and reduced reproductive function
> -Miscarriages
> -Parkinson's disease [28]

Again, do you want any of these things listed to happen to you or your family? WE must eat to live, not eat to die. Right now in America we are literally eating ourselves to death. Food can be an addiction just like drugs and alcohol. Processed toxic foods are even more likely to become addictions, because the chemicals used in them hold addictive properties. We all have to eat, so it is important to choose wisely. If you knew and understood half of what you probably put in your body everyday, and the damage that it is doing to you health wise, I can almost guarantee you would not eat the same things anymore. It comes down to education, plain and simple. Education gives you the knowledge and power to make better choices. I love what my friend Minta Allred says. Minta is a raw foodist, and one of the healthiest people I know. She says, " I never count calories, I only read ingredients." If you care about yourself, your body, and life, then you must become educated about it. To learn more about Minta and eating raw foods you can visit her site at www.mintaallred.com

Many people say that price is the main issue when deciding to purchase organic vs. non-organic foods. A lot of people say to me, I would eat organic foods more if I could afford to. Well, my answer is, you absolutely can afford to. How could you not? What is more expensive, having a life threatening health disease, or spending an extra twenty to fifty cents on an organic item? The truth is, that when we shop we are voting. Every single time you buy something at the store you are casting your vote. You are voting for processed or fresh, organic or non-organic, gmo or non-gmo. If you demand to buy organic high quality foods then you would get that. If every one of us put up a stink about the price of organic foods, and used our voices to propel change, things would be a lot different in this country. There are more of us then the people that run these major corporations. We are more powerful than we could ever imagine, but we have been programmed to act like sheep. We are not sheep. We are humans. It is our God given right to have good clean food.

Not Milk?

One of the other problems within the food industry is the dairy industry. We are a culture obsessed with dairy. We have been taught from an early age on that milk does a body good. This is an absolute lie. The dairy industry is tied into the regular food industry, which is also tied into these major corporations. They are all connected, and all work closely together to keep the public from knowing the truth. Let's take a look at milk. I personally do not drink milk. Unless we are a baby calf, we don't need to be drinking milk. We are the only mammals that still consume milk past the age of four, and that also drink the milk from another mammal. We wouldn't even think about drinking dog's milk, cat's milk, or any other milk that came from a nursing mammal. So why do we find it so appetizing to drink cows milk? It is because it has been marketed to us that way, and we have never questioned it. Milk is supposed to be good for building strong bones, giving us calcium, and making us grow up strong. This could not be farther from the reality. Not only is the milk we drink in America coming from a polluted source, but also, there are all sorts of bacteria, and even puss found in our milk. This is due to the way our cows are treated. There are many reasons why I believe this beverage is toxic and not good for us. Here are a few.

> 1. Milk in the U. S. comes from cows that are regularly pumped with hormones, steroids, and antibiotics, they are fed corn instead of grass, and their living conditions are criminal. If you don't believe me, just watch Food.inc or go on PETA's website www.peta.org

> 2. According to Robert Kradjian, MD, in his letter to his patients telling them not to drink milk he states that. "Fifty years ago an average cow produced 2,000 pounds of milk per year. Today the top producers give 50,000 pounds! How was this accomplished? Drugs, antibiotics, hormones, forced feeding plans and specialized breeding; that's how. The latest high-tech onslaught on the poor cow is bovine growth hormone or BGH. This genetically engineered drug is supposed to stimulate milk production but, according to Monsanto, the hormone's manufacturer, does not affect the milk or meat. There are three other manufacturers: Upjohn, Eli Lilly, and American Cyanamid Company. Obviously, there have been no long-term studies on the hormone's effect on the humans drinking the milk. Other countries have banned BGH because of safety concerns. 3.70% of the world's population does not drink milk. Why? Because it literally makes them ill. Unless you are a young calf, you don't need to be consuming Milk. "[29]

> 3. Consuming Milk regularly can actually increase your chances of osteoporosis not the other way around. In fact, the countries with the highest dairy consumption such as the U. S. and Denmark, have the highest rates of osteoporosis in the world. This happens because a diet filled with too much protein, which can cause the body to become acidic and leach

calcium out of the bones. According to PETA, "American women consume tremendous amounts of calcium, their rates of osteoporosis are among the highest in the world. Conversely, Chinese people consume half as much calcium (most of it from plant sources) and have a very low incidence of the bone disease. Medical studies indicate that rather than preventing the disease, milk may actually increase women's risk of getting osteoporosis. " A Harvard Nurses' Study of more than 77,000 women ages 34 to 59 found that those who consumed two or more glasses of milk per day had higher risks of broken hips and arms than those who drank one glass or less per day. T. Colin Campbell, professor of nutritional biochemistry at Cornell University, said, "The association between the intake of animal protein and fracture rates appears to be as strong as that between cigarette smoking and lung cancer." [30]

4. Peta's research also states that "According to Dr. Frank Oski, the former director of pediatrics at Johns Hopkins University, "There is no reason to drink cow's milk at any time in your life. It was designed for calves, it was not designed for humans, and we should all stop drinking it today, this afternoon."[13] Dr. Spock agreed, saying, "There was a time when cow's milk was considered very desirable. But research, along with clinical experience, has forced doctors and nutritionists to rethink this recommendation." [31]

5. The biggest myth is that you have to drink Milk to get calcium, Vitamin D, and protein. You can get more absorbable calcium and even protein from eating green leafy vegetables in raw and natural juice form, and you can get your Vitamin D naturally from the sun. You do not need Milk for health.

"Osteoporosis is caused by a number of things, one of the most important being too much dietary protein."
{Science 1986;233, 4763}

The other issue I have with milk is that, because so many people are allergic too it and may not know that they are, it can contribute to other heath issues, especially in children. According to Natural News,

> "up to half of all infants may be sensitive to cows' milk. As a result, symptoms of an underlying milk allergy may start as early as infancy, only manifested as eczema, a symptom that may remain later on in childhood and adulthood. Furthermore, in addition to asthma and eczema, an underlying milk allergy may manifest as bronchitis, sinusitis, autoimmune disorders, frequent colds and ear infections and even behavioral problems."[32]

So now that we have looked at some of the factors of why milk is not the best choice for us, let us take a look at the cost of milk vs. a healthier alternative. The average cost of cow's milk is about $3.50 a gallon vs. organic almond milk priced at $3.98 a gallon. Is your health worth an extra 48 cents to you? I don't know maybe it is not, but if you have read this far, I am going to think that you care about yourself and your family. There are several healthy alternatives to cow's milk that are much more nutritious and even affordable. Almond Milk, Coconut Milk, and even Hemp Seed Milk are all fantastic choices for your health. I personally get my organic almond milk at Trader Joe's for $1.99 for a 32oz container. I do not give my daughters regular milk. I nursed for a year, and then went straight to almond, coconut, and some goat's milk. Goat's milk has a much closer amino acid and nutrient profile to that of human breast milk so it can be a good option when weaning a baby off of breast milk. For my youngest daughter she didn't like almond milk at first so I would mix a small amount of organic goat's milk into the almond milk to get her used to it. Goat's milk is a much cleaner source than regular cow milk. The only thing you need to watch out for in dairy alternative milks is an ingredient called carrageenan.

It is a food additive present in a lot of vegan and non-dairy health foods. According to the Cornucopia Institute, carrageenan, which is derived from red seaweed, has a multitude of potential health risks for humans.

> "For the past four decades, scientists have warned that the use of carrageenan in food is not safe. Animal studies have repeatedly shown that food-grade carrageenan causes gastrointestinal inflammation and higher rates of intestinal lesions, ulcerations, and even malignant tumors." [33]

Even vegan health products are not safe from the food industry demons anymore. You must learn to always read labels and learn ingredients. It is the only way we can truly protect ourselves anymore.

My one and only exception to traditional cow milk products in our house are the Isa Lean Isagenix shakes. The Isa Lean Isagenix shakes are made from organic whey proteins from a private family farm in New Zealand. The cows are grass fed, not corn fed like here in the US. They have never been treated with drugs or antibiotics, and the proteins are extracted from the milk in a way that ensures the nutritional content of the amino acid. It is, undenatured, which means it is not heated to high temperatures, and the enzymes are not killed. It is 98% lactose free, and is not even considered a dairy product. To me, the nutritional content we receive from these shakes far out ways any negative effect of the small amount of milk proteins that are in it. Plus, Isagenix has just released a new Dairy-Free/Vegan Isa Lean shake and my girls and I have just switched over to that. For more information on this vegan super food shake go to the **ECEG.**

It is highly important if you choose to still eat dairy, to consume as much organic dairy as possible. This will at least diminish some of the impurities that you are exposed to. Although, you will still be susceptible to the other negative effects of dairy if you do choose to eat it.

It is not your fault that you don't know these things. You have been programmed and conditioned by the media, parents, and friends to believe Milk is ok for you to consume. My absolute hope is that, some of this information will stick. That some of the things I am revealing to you will make you start to question current beliefs you may have, so that, you can revisit them to see if they are serving you and benefiting your life. I truly believe that people want to be healthy and feel good, they just don't know how, and they are too tired, sick, and confused to search for the answers. When in doubt go back to nature, go back to our beginnings and do what we did for thousands of years before our modernization started to take over and kill us.

It is funny to me because when I am talking to a new client and helping them get on a super food program, a common question is usually, 'Well, what is in this stuff?' I always reply by saying, its just food. Sometimes people are so concerned about putting something in their bodies that can actually be good for them, but they don't think twice about popping open a Diet Coke or pulling through the drive through. Again, when in doubt, look back to nature, look to the ground and the elements for the answers to health. Do not look to drugs and synthetic compounds to cure you. Your body is a miracle and through real foods and proper nutrition it can regenerate; and yes, it can heal itself!

Research has shown that fast food and junk food habits are equally as addictive as that of heroine and cocaine. According to a study done at Scripps Research Institute in Florida, they found that laboratory rats became addicted to a bad diet just like they became dependant on cocaine and heroin. It actually had the same effect on the brain. Dr Paul Kenny, a neuroscientist who led the research, said the study, which took nearly three years to complete, confirmed the "addictive" properties of junk food. "It presents the most thorough and compelling evidence that drug addiction and obesity are based on the same underlying neurobiological mechanisms." The research indicated that the junk food altered the chemical balance in the parts of the brain that handle the feel-good chemical dopamine, or the rewards center of the brain. Identical changes happened in the brains of rats given cocaine or heroin, and these areas are thought to play a key role in drug addiction. [34] Again, why is this not front-page news!!

My question to all the parents out there is, would you give heroin or cocaine to your children or to anyone you care about for that matter? I would hope your answer would be absolutely not! Then, why are we feeding our children this disgraceful food? I believe that one day it will be considered child abuse to feed your children fast food, just like it would be considered child abuse if you fed them alcohol or drugs. In my opinion there is no difference, and science and research are showing us that biologically there really is no difference. I hope you can see that putting real foods in your body is vitally important to your health and life. Our culture has literally become a clan of processed people and we have to break this unfortunate and devastating cycle so we can live our true potential.

Chapter 4

Breaking The Toxic Cycle

Now that you are aware of some of the health risks facing you and your family, it is time to take a look at some of the ways we can break the toxic cycle. When I was pregnant for the first time with my daughter I knew I had an undeniable responsibility to put good things in my body so that she could form and function properly. A lot of women take care of their bodies when they are pregnant, but after the baby is born they go back to their old unhealthy habits. The issue is, that even after our children are born they are constantly learning from us and modeling our behavior. If Mom and Dad eat junk food or smoke, they become accustomed to seeing this as 'normal behavior' and may repeat the cycle. If we want to change the state of our health in this country we must start to break the cycle. The cycle starts at home, and you are in control of it.

In the October 2010 issue of Time Magazine, the leading article was titled 'How the First Nine Months Shape Your Life.' In this article, written by Annie Murphy Paul, she brilliantly depicts the new advances in science about the importance of nutrition in utero.

> "The quality of nutrition you received in the womb; the pollutants, drugs, and infections you were exposed to during gestation; your mother's health, stress level and state of mind while she was pregnant with you—all of these factors shaped you as a baby and a child and continue to affect you to this day." This new scientific field known as fetal origins is giving us amazing insights into how important nutrition and health are even before a baby is born. This research indicates that the conditions we experience in utero help to shape and predetermine our

susceptibility to disease and illness. It is also linked to our appetite, metabolism, intelligence levels and even our attitudes. "Much of what a pregnant woman encounters in her daily life, the air she breathes, the food and drink she consumes, the chemicals she's exposed to, even the emotions she feels-is shared in some fashion with her fetus. The fetus incorporates these offerings into this own body, makes them part of its flesh and blood." [35]

The article also discussed the findings of a Harvard Medical Study that indicated that a women's weight gain during pregnancy could affect the weight gain of the child later in life. One study even found that the higher the weight gain, the higher the chance of the child becoming overweight by the age of three. Another devastating factor was the amount of toxicity the mother was exposed to just from the air alone. In 1998 they did a study of 500 pregnant women who wore backpacks with air monitors in them to test the levels of PAH's (polycyclic aromatic hydrocarbons). These toxins come from anything that burns; fuel, cigarette smoke, and factories. The findings were that 100% of the women were exposed to these toxins during their pregnancy. The sad part was that 40% of the infants showed they had small amounts of DNA damage from these chemicals that have been linked to an increased risk of cancer, and were twice as likely to be cognitively delayed at age three. The most pressing part of this article to me was the research revealed by the Linus Pauling Institute. David Williams, who is a chief investigator at this institute, is "testing the notions that certain substances consumed during pregnancy can provide offspring with lifelong chemo protection from illness. In William's studies, the offspring of mice that ingested a pytochemical derived from cruciferous vegetables like broccoli and cabbage during pregnancy were much less likely to get cancer, even when exposed to a known carcinogen. After they were weaned, the offspring never encountered these protective chemicals again, yet their exposure shielded them from cancer well into maturity. He predicts that one day, pregnant women will be prescribed a dietary supplement that will protect their future children from cancer." [34]

Wow, so by eating certain high quality vegetables, or supplements during pregnancy we may be able to protect our children from diseases like cancer later on in life, even when they are exposed to the known carcinogens that we encounter daily! This research and article is so profound at showing the importance of proper nutrition, and also proper cleansing of the system. We know we are going to be exposed to chemicals daily, but if we properly take care of our immune systems through nutrition and lifestyle we can minimize these effects. I have cleansed regularly through each of my pregnancies to diminish the amount of toxins that can affect the baby. You cannot do a deep full cleanse while pregnant but you can do certain forms of daily cleansing.

We have to start breaking the cycle starting with pregnancy. If a woman eats a balanced diet during pregnancy her moods stay level, her weight gain does not get out of control, and her child is better protected and able to grow properly. The minute a woman finds out she is pregnant the cycle starts. It will either be a healthy positive cycle or a toxic negative one. It is my goal to help as many pregnant women as possible get the proper nutrition, keep their weight balanced, and have a happy and healthy pregnancy. If I can do it, I know you can do it too!

Be The Example

Our kids want to eat good foods, they just don't know how unless you show them. A lot of parents ask me how I get my kids to eat raw veggies and healthy foods. My answer is always, "Because

I give it to them, and it is all they have ever known." I would never feed my child McDonald's because I know too much about what is in it. Once you become aware of the reality, you will automatically make a shift. Children do not need to eat french fries and drink soda, just like they don't need to be doing drugs and drinking alcohol. That may sound a bit harsh but it really isn't. Fast food is poison, so are drugs, period. Why should it be different? Because we have been lied to by the marketing campaigns of these companies? Please, we are smarter than that, aren't we? Fast food companies have targeted children and adolescents for years. According to Natural News, soda companies even went as far as branding labels to resemble soda cans on baby bottles.

> "PepsiCo company began branding plastic baby bottles with soft drink logos in the 1990's, hoping that parents would begin feeding their infants and babies soft drinks such as Pepsi and Mountain Dew.
> Once again, many people find this very difficult to believe and they think we're just making this up. But of course, we're not: Check out the February 1, 1996 issue of Pediatrics for Parents, which contains the following published report:
> Soft drink manufacturers are now putting their logos on baby bottles. The logos of many carbonated drinks (Pepsi, diet and regular; 7 Up: Dr. Pepper; Orange Slice: and Mountain Dew), non-carbonated drinks (Kool-Aid), and juice drinks (Mott's; Welch's; Very Fine; V8; and Perrier) can be seen on plastic baby bottles.
> Health experts are concerned over this trend. They fear that parents will be encouraged to give their babies inappropriate beverages in their baby bottles. In a study of 314 California mothers, almost a third admitted to giving their baby's either soft drinks or Kool-Aid. Over half had baby bottles with soda, Kool-Aid, or juice logos." [36]

McDonald's has used their famous icon Ronald McDonald to lure kids into their facilities. Coca Cola has used images of Santa for years to promote their drinks. Every major fast food chain promotes and endorses the newest films for children promising free gifts with a purchase of their kids or "happy meals". It is estimated that 90% of children visit McDonald's once a month! Only one of the "happy meals" meets the calorie guideline for children. Fast food chains tie in advertising of new movies for children with the star characters. This evokes the same emotions that children feel when watching these films and lures them to want to get these toys, and thus eat at these restaurants. They also use specific colors in their marketing, packaging, and signs. Fast food chains use to the color red because it represents warmth, fresh food, meat, and action. It is also an appetite enhancer. Yellow is used to create a welcoming atmosphere. Yellow is also associated with cheerfulness and actually evokes the feel good centers of the brain. Think of all the major fast food chains. What color are their signs and marketing? They are all red and yellow. McDonald's, Wendy's, Carl's Jr, Sonic, Burger King, In and Out, KooKoRoo, and many others have used these main colors. These corporations are smart, they know what they are doing, and they know how to control the masses.

My advice to you and for the safety of your family is to become an educated consumer. Take your power back, and take a stand against this corruption. A lot of people think that I am over the top with my views. While I am passionate about these subjects, I do not think putting up a fight for our health and for our children is being over the top. If you knew that people where being led into a corral to be poisoned to death, would you not stand at the gate trying to stop them from going in? That is how I feel about the food industry. We have to stand in front of the corral, jump, and scream, and try to talk some sense into the people that are just blindly walking into be slaughtered. It is a horrible image, but it is essentially the truth of what is going on.

To break the cycle, we must first become educated about the truth. I applaud you for taking the time to read this far. That tells me that you are a person of integrity, and that you want a better life for yourself and your family. Second, we must join the crusade and start to share this vital information with others. And third, we must be constantly aware of the things we are purchasing because when we buy things we vote for what we want. Becoming an educated and empowered consumer is not easy. This takes time, research, and a commitment to health. That is part of the reason I wrote this book. I want people to have a guide and a starting point to have some education that will inspire them to learn more. I am constantly reading new studies, articles, and postings from people involved in this crusade. I surround myself with people that know more about these subjects than I do, so that I can learn more. If this is the only thing you ever read about health, then at least you learned a little bit. I would encourage you to get involved with organizations that promote this sort of education. Join Meet Ups, Facebook groups, subscribe to daily emails from organizations like the Organic Consumers Association, Slow Foods, and Food Matters. To see some of the organizations I am apart of and donate to, you can visit my website at www.yourlifedetoxed.com or go to the **ECEG.** You can also sign up to receive my FREE weekly emails called "Messages From Your Body" where I give out a ton of free nutrition information, recipes and more. To sign up go to www.brittneykara.wordpress.com

There are literally thousands of articles, publications, and downloads that can help you get educated about the most important thing in your life, your health. I love what I do with my work in Isagenix because I get to help educate so many people about these concepts.

Whether I am doing a one on one consultation, or I am speaking to a room full of people, I always feel good inside knowing I may be helping to change someone's life that day. When I receive emails and phone calls from people thanking me for saving or changing their lives, I feel so humbled. I know that I am truly living into my purpose, and that I am helping to break the negative toxic cycle. My husband is a firefighter, and he gets to save lives everyday. I could never do what he does, therefore, I never thought I would have the opportunity to save and change lives. I feel blessed and humbled to have an opportunity now to share this information with you. When you change your life, you unconsciously give others the right to change theirs. I believe that is why we are all here on this planet, to make a difference, to help each other, and to affect change. While there is a lot of negativity surrounding us right now in our world, there is also a global shift of consciousness that is going to make things better. People are starting to wake up to some of the injustices, and are banding together to make a difference. I hope you will join us!

One Angry Chick

When I first started blogging and writing about these topics I had created this alter ego type character called, One Angry Chick. As I mentioned earlier this blog was the catalyst for writing this book. I saw that people were upset just like I was and they wanted answers and guidance about their health. Creating One Angry Chick (OAC) allowed me to fight for a cause that I strongly believe in. I want to have a worldwide army of Angry Chicks and Angry Dudes, out there changing the world through education and inspiration. Together we can change the food and health industry forever, and save future generations from a catastrophic downfall. Napoleon

Hill said, "Whatever the mind of man can believe and conceive he can achieve." I think he really meant to say 'Whatever the mind of an angry chick on a mission to change the health of a nation can believe and conceive she can achieve!' but I will let him slide on that. I have a vision of smart, healthy, vibrant people all over the world, getting along and loving each other. Call me idealistic or a dreamer, or whatever you want, but I can see it in my mind. Therefore, I know it is possible to create it. The problem is I can't do it on my own. Dr Mercola and Natural News can't do it on their own, Isagenix, and the organic farm industry can't do it on their own. We have to all band together to create the largest community ever. We have to fight, and we have to be heard. We deserve to have our God given rights, we deserve to live long healthy lives, we deserve to have good clean foods, we deserve to have sound and just medical advice, we deserve to have options to cancer therapies, we deserve to raise our children in the healthiest way possible, we deserve to not be pumped full of drugs and antibiotics, and we deserve to be treated like the amazing human beings that we are. If you don't say something, you may not ever be heard. So use your voice, use your power, and remember that everyone has a right to the best quality of life possible.

Breaking the cycle is necessary for us all to move past this and become empowered. It is our God given right to have good clean foods in our bodies, and it is also our right to know what is being done to our food before we eat it. We cannot walk around like zombies anymore. We must wake up and fight. I have received dozens of phone calls from people I have coached through nutritional cleansing, and one of the first things people usually say to me, is 'I feel like I have been in a haze, and my mind is being clear now to my reality'. From that point on they automatically start making healthier choices and empowering themselves to learn more. When the mind becomes clear of all the junk, we start to feel better and we can function at our optimal level of health. It is not normal to be sick and tired all the time, yet most people are living their lives in a state of survival. I say that it is time to go from surviving to thriving. The most important step to getting there is to detoxify the body. Everything leading up to this point has shown us why we need to detoxify and cleanse away the toxins. In the next chapter I am going to show you how to do this.

Chapter 5

Cleanse to Live: How to properly detoxify your body and life

Let me ask you a question; do you shower everyday? Do you brush your teeth? Do you get regular check ups at the dentist? I hope you answered yes to those questions. We do those things without even thinking about it, because we know we have to. If we did not clean our bodies everyday we would smell bad and no one would want to be around us. If we didn't brush our teeth, they would rot and fall out. We do all of these steps to maintain the outside of our bodies to make sure everything is looking good, yet we forget about what is most important, our insides. Our internal body is much more important than the external. Just because we can't see if it is getting dirty, or corroded with stuff, doesn't mean that it isn't. In fact, it absolutely is. Our bodies endure so much, everyday. Think about all the things we have been talking about. All the toxins, poisons, chemicals, preservatives, and junk we flood our bodies with daily. Yet, we never stop to think about cleaning out the inside. Cleansing and detoxing has been around for thousands of years. Many ancient cultures used cleansing and herbs to heal the body and to maintain a state of balance. It has been a tradition among humans throughout all cultures and ages. It was even a way to connect with the Divine in ancient times. Cleansing and detox is talked about it the Bible, and most major religions around the world. Cleansing has become essential now, more so than ever, for us to just stay healthy and survive. Cleansing is just like showering on the inside of your body. It is not something you should do from time to time. It is something we must all do regularly to protect ourselves.

Many people are afraid of cleansing because of a lack of education about it and what it entails. Many people think of things such as coffee enemas, colonics, and fasts as the only form of cleansing. While there are many different types of cleansing and cleanses out there, I am going to speak to you about the safest, most effective way to cleanse your body. It is called Nutritional Cleansing. Nutritional Cleansing is a way for your body to get a well-deserved break, and to naturally start to remove impurities from the organs and cells. This type of cleansing is not a fast because it is flooding your body with organic nutrients, herbal teas, and minerals. Your body is actually still getting nutrition without having to break down and digest solid foods. The best way to give your body a break is to do this. Not only will your body function better, but also you will have more energy, metal clarity, and the side benefit of nutritional cleansing is weight loss. Let's talk about why so many people lose weight with nutritional cleansing.

First of all, when you go on a traditional diet, you restrict your caloric intake. When this happens you minimize your fat intake and your fat cells start to shrink. There is one problem though. Remember all the poisons and toxins? Where do those go in your body? Believe it or not they actually hide out in your fat cells and vital organs. Your liver's job is to protect you from these impurities. When toxins enter your body, from air, food, and water, your body's natural defense is to cover them with excess water and fat. Your body will manufacture more fat cells for the amount of toxicity you have in your system. So when you go on a diet, you restrict your calories, your fat cells shrink, and out pop the toxins. You then become a walking time bomb because your body is filled with so many impurities. What does your body do next? It covers them back up. This is why 98% of diets fail. They are not dealing with the real issue, toxicity. Not to mention that most 'diet foods' are toxic already. They are usually frozen, highly processed, and often contain the "sugar free" substances we discussed earlier that are very unhealthy. When you properly cleanse the body, you properly lose weight. Cleansing allows the cells to open up, releasing and flushing out the toxins, so the extra fat and water can dissipate. When you cleanse, you not only lose the unwanted fat and inches, but you also gain hydration in your cells, known as intra cellular water. Extra cellular water is the bad water that can makes us feel puffy and balloted. Intra cellular water is what our cells need for proper functionality.

Through cleansing, the systems of your body can get relief and start to regenerate properly. This is the best way to allow the body to heal itself. The human body is designed to heal itself, but for the most part we do not give it enough time, or the proper components for it to do this. Through nutritional cleansing all of this can be accomplished.

Many people cleanse on a seasonal basis. I used to be one of those people until I discovered Nutritional Cleansing. I have been doing different kinds of cleansing and studying cleansing for the past fifteen years. The cleansing systems I used to use where very tough on the system, they were time consuming, and worse yet, they tasted horrible. I would just choke down whatever the concoction was because I knew that my body was getting clean so it was worth it. When I found Isagenix, my cleansing education went to a whole other level. Isagenix actually has the, first and only, full body nutritional cleanse. What that means is that it cleanses all of your vital organs and cells at the same time, but it is also a high quality super food that is feeding the body on a cellular level. That means that you are never starving the body. In fact, 2-4 oz a day of this cleanse juice is equal to 14-18 servings or organic fruits and vegetables antioxidant wise for the body! Not only do you get that power packed punch of nutrition, but it tastes amazing too. Because the body doesn't go into starvation mode, you do not mess up your metabolism. It actually increases your metabolic rate, helps to balance your blood sugars, gives you incredible energy and mental clarity, removes deadly toxins, and helps with weight loss. It has anti-aging properties in it as well that promote vitality and longevity of your cells. This cleanse is very gentle on the system and is not designed to blow you out. In fact, it stimulates your lymphatic system and allows you to pee out most of your toxins. You can use this cleanse on a daily basis, or do a deep cleanse a few times a month depending on what your health goals are. For people that need to lose weight, doing a cleanse day once a week until they reach their goal would be ideal. You can even do a two day deep cleanse that really helps to get the system balanced and moving properly. After a two day deep cleanse I always feel rejuvenated, energized and amazing! You know that wonderful feeling you get when you hop out of a nice hot shower? That is how I feel after a good cleanse day. The best part is, you are not starving. There are several components of the cleansing program that you can eat, including organic dark super chocolates called Isa Delights, which I mentioned in the super food section. These little treats are so decadent, and they are loaded with nutrition. Just one chocolate has the antioxidant value of a whole basket of blueberries! So literally I always tell people that they can lose weight in a healthy way by eating chocolate! How fun is that?

Nutritional cleansing is so vital to our health for all of the reasons we have been discussing. Once you cleanse out all the bad stuff, it is time to replenish your body with the proper nutrients and super foods. Once your cells are not dirty anymore they can absorb the nutrition better. There are many professional athletes that swear by this philosophy because it allows their bodies to recover better, and also allows their muscles to absorb proteins faster. You can put on a tremendous amount of lean muscle mass when the body is clean and you are putting clean sources of protein back in. You can remember what happened to my friend Nick and his incredible transformation on Isagenix. The phenomenal thing about John Anderson's creation with the Isagenix system is that all of this is done for you. The programs are specifically designed to give your body all of these components, so it takes the guess work out. I used to boil herbs, chop dozens of raw garlic cubes, spend ours juicing organic fruits and vegetables, just to try to get the benefit of what nutritional cleansing allows me to do. Now all I do is open the fridge and take a shot or a glass full of Cleanse For Life and my work is done. My body knows what to do with the nutrition, and I just get to reap all the benefits. Not only do I save time and money, but also my house doesn't smell like a science experiment gone wrong.

Cleansing helps the body regain balance in all areas. A lot of people tell me after they have done a deep cleanse that they even see colors more vividly. I definitely notice a difference in my taste buds after I have cleansed. I am much more aware of the sodium content in foods and also how sweet things are. One of my holistic doctor friends says that a healthy clean body craves healthy clean foods, but a dirty body craves dirty foods. That statement could not be more accurate. When you're clean on the inside you look and feel great on the outside. We can figure out if our bodies are clean or dirty just by paying attention to what we are craving. If you are craving junk you need to cleanse. Basic cleansing should be done daily, and deep cleansing should be done monthly depending on where you are starting from. If you are overweight or have some health problems, you will need to do deeper cleansing more often until your body gets balanced again. The more you cleanse, the better you get at it, and the more you enjoy how you feel. Just like anything else in life, you must be consistent to see results.

I always recommend cleansing with a friend. We do all sorts of group cleanses and accountability groups to keep people on track for their success. When you have a support system in place, and you have people around you helping you get educated it can make these life changes easier. Maintaining a cleansing lifestyle, while it is essential to your health, is a personal choice. Just because you cleanse regularly does not mean you do not eat regular foods or can't enjoy life. I love cleansing, and I also love to eat the foods I enjoy and drink a glass of wine if I want. You can find a balance of these lifestyles and make them work for you. Cleansing is internal hygiene; it is necessary for us to thrive optimally. Just like other forms of personal hygiene, everyone has their own way of making things work. We have certain guidelines in place that we know about, and then we do what is right for us and what makes us feel good. Just like personal hygiene cleansing is an essential part of my life. I will always shower, brush my teeth, and cleanse, period.

I hope that as you start your health journey you will continue to educate yourself on the other material that is out there. Like I mentioned earlier, this is about you, about exposing you to something that I believe you should be aware of, and then implementing this new information into your life so *you* can thrive. Most Americans are in survival mode with their health, and other aspects of their lives. My goal and passion is to assist people to move outside of the surviving box and go into a place where they can thrive. Cleansing is a huge part of that because it allows us to remove the junk from our bodies, regain our health, and thus remove the junk from our lives.

The Price of Beauty- Skin and Body Care Basics

Once you have cleansed your body, it is time to detoxify the other aspects of your life. Another main source of toxins comes from the products we put on our skin. This is especially true for women, because, 83 percent of all cosmetics contain cancer-causing ingredients. Anything you put on your skin filters through your liver in about a thirty- minute period, sometimes faster, depending on your system. Your skin is the largest organ in your body and you soak in toxins every time you take a shower, bathe, put lotions on, makeup, and perfumes. Most people drink filtered water, but most people do not bathe in filtered water. This is a huge health issue and it can be solved very easily. For example, just adding an outside filter on the house you live in can filter your bathing water. If you live in an apartment you can get a filter that fits onto your showerhead. These are relatively inexpensive and range between $35-$150 depending on the brand. This is important, because again, we have to bathe, and we also need to diminish our toxic exposure. Since most beauty and personal care products contain toxic ingredients that are deadly to our health it is important to look into this a bit further.

As far as our daily personal hygiene goes, there are specific ingredients that I recommend people stay away from. Here is a list of some common chemicals found in almost all the beauty products you probably have in your cabinet right now that have toxic effects on the body. Although the list is long, don't let it overwhelm you. Just make a choice and concentrate on changing one thing at a time. Of course, the government does not require labeling or health studies on ingredients used in personal care products, so yet again, it is our job to get educated. For more detailed information on specific products you can visit the Environmental Working Group's website at www.ewg.org or go to your ECEG.

- Acetone - Found in nail polish remover.
- Acetaldehyde - Found in many nail care products.
- Alkyl-phenol Ethoxylades - Found in shampoo and bubble bath.
- Aluminum - Found in antiperspirant deodorants and antiseptics.
- Ammonium Glycolate - Found in body products.
- Ammonium Per sulfate - Found in hair color and bleaching kits
- Aspartame - Found in some body products, such as shaving cream
- Benzyl/Benzene - Used in pharmaceutical drugs, cosmetics, shower gels, shampoos, and bubble bath.
- BHT - Found in body products.
- Bronopol - Found in body products.
- Carboxymethylcellulose - Used in cosmetics.
- Coal Tar Dyes (includes FD&C, D&C Blue 1, Green 3, Yellow 5, Yellow 6, Yellow 11, Red 33, etc.) - Found in bubble bath, hair dye, bath oil/salts/soak, body spray, moisturizer, lip gloss, polish remover, nail polish lipstick, styling gel/lotion, bar soap, after sun products, cologne, nail treatment, dandruff shampoo, cosmetics and toothpaste.
- Collagen – Found in body and skin products (derived from animal skins and chicken feet).
- Coumadin - Used in the manufacturing of deodorants, shampoos, skin fresheners and perfumes.
- DEA (diethanolamine), MEA (monoethanolamine), & TEA (methanolamine) - Usually listed on the label as Cocamide DEA -CETYL phosphates or MEA, Lauramide DEA, Stearamide MEA, Linoleamide Tea, Myristamide DEA, Triethanolamine DEA, Oleamide DEA, TEA-Lauryl Sulfate etc. These are almost always in skin cream, cosmetics, bubble bath, shaving gel, hairsprays, sunscreens, conditioner, lotions, and prod-

ucts that foam, including bubble baths, body washes, shampoos, soaps and facial cleansers.

• DEET – Found in insect repellent.

• Dibutyl phthalate (DBP) - Found in nail polish. This is banned in Europe, but is still used in US.

• Dioforms - Found in tooth whitening products.

• Elastin - Found in facial creams and body lotions.

• Ethylacrylate - Found in some mascaras.

• Fluoride - Found in toothpastes.

• Formaldehyde - Found in nail care products, baby shampoo, bubble bath, deodorants, perfume, cologne, hair dye, mouthwash, toothpaste, hair spray.

• Fragrances (Synthetic) – Found in perfumes/fragrances, shampoos, most deodorants, sunscreens, skin care, body care and baby products.

• Glycolic Acid - Found in creams, lotions, and cosmetics.

• Hydroabietyl Alcohol - Found in styling gel and lotions.

• Hydroquinone - Found in skin lightening products and hair dyes.

• Hydroxymethylcellulose - Used in cosmetics.

• Imidazolidinyl urea and DM hydantoine - Common in nearly all skin, body and hair care products, antiperspirants and nail polish.

• Isoproponal/Isopropyl Alcohol - Found in some body products, mouthwash, toothpaste, cleansers, hair color rinses, body rubs, hand lotions, fragrances, hair dyes, massage oils, hand creams, after shave lotions, perfumes and many other cosmetic products.

Kajoic Acid - Used in skin lightening products.

•Lacquer - Found in mascara.

•Lanolin - Found in body products.

•Lye - Found in bars of soap.

- Magnesium Stearate - Used in talcum powder.
- Methylisothiazoline or MIT - Found in shampoo.
- Methyl Methacrylate - Found in nail polish.
- Mineral Oil - Found in blush, baby oil which is 100% mineral oil, lotions, foundation and creams.
- NDEA - Often used in cosmetics to adjust the pH, and used with many fatty acids to convert acid to salt (stearate), which then becomes the base for a cleanser.
- Nitrosamines and Padimate-O (PABA) - Found in cosmetics and sunscreens.
- Parabens (methyl, propyl-, butyl-, Isobutyl- and ethyl-) - Widely used in beauty and body products.
- Paraffin - Found in cosmetics.
- Petroleum (Petrolatum), Petrolatum and Paraffin Gel (petroleum jelly) - Found in lotions, skin creams, and body jelly.
- Phthalates - Found in perfume, hair spray, deodorant, nail polish, hair gel, mousse, body and hand lotion. Usually not listed on label, banned in Europe but still used in the US.
- Polypropylene - Found in lipstick, mascara, baby soap, and eye shadow.
- Polyquaternium-7 - Found in body products.
- Propylene Glycol - Found in shaving gel, lotions, shampoo, conditioners, deodorant, most forms of make-up, hair products, after-shave, mouthwashes and toothpaste.
- PVP/VA Copolymere - Used in shampoos and conditioners.
- Quaternium-7, 15, 31, 60 etc. - Found in body products
- Sodium Chloride - Found in shampoo as a thickener.
- Sodium Hydroxymethylglycinate - Found in facial moisturizer, facial cleanser, facial treatments, skin

fading and lightening products, anti-aging products, eye makeup remover, concealer, makeup remover, around eye cream, acne treatment, shampoo, conditioner, styling lotion and gel, styling mousse and foam, hair spray, hair relaxer, tanning oil and sunscreen, after tanning products, body cleanser and wash, body exfoliates, body firming lotion, baby soap, baby lotion, baby wipes, baby bubble bath, pain and wound products, hand sanitizer.

•SLS (Sodium Lauryl Sulphate) & SLES (Sodium Laureth Sulphate) - May be labeled natural or even organic and found in toothpaste, soap, cosmetics, shampoo, body wash, bubble bath, facial cleansers, hair conditioners.

• Stearalkonium Chloride - Used in hair conditioners and in skin creams.

•Talc - Found in blush, condoms, baby powder, feminine powders, deodorant, foot and body powders.

•Toluene - Found in nail polish, and cleaning products.

•Triclosan - Found in a lot of antimicrobial soap, antibacterial soap, deodorants, cosmetics, lotions, creams, and even toothpaste products, it can react with chlorine in the tap water to create Chloroform. A safe, non-toxic alternative that has many applications is Grapefruit Seed Extract.

•Zinc Stearate - Found in blush and powder foundation.

Deodorant was the hardest for me. I went through probably 25 or more types of natural deodorant before I found one that works for me. I now use a natural crystal, and it is great. Recently I found a great non-toxic deodorant at Sephora. I was presently surprised to see a product like that in a big chain beauty store. As consumers start to demand more organic and natural products at mainstream stores we will start seeing these options in more and more traditional stores. Again, you are voting every time you shop! You see it is actually up to us, not them. The consumer can dictate the market and make a product flourish or fail.

As I started to get rid of toxic ingredients in my body products, I did go through a period where my body was detoxifying the years of aluminum that had been shoved in my armpit. I am not going to lie to you; you will probably smell bad in the very beginning as your body releases impurities. The more I cleansed my body and drank a lot of water, the quicker the body odor went away. I always thought of it this way; would I rather have a little body odor for a few weeks or get breast cancer and possibly lose my boobs? I opted for the first option. Again the more you cleanse your body, the healthier you will be and the less you will have any types of body odor.

I also use natural toothpaste that does not contain fluoride. Fluoride is a toxic chemical that actually can cause tooth decay. Again, it is just like dealing with the pharmaceuticals and the ADA makes a lot of money off of people getting fillings in their mouth. Fluoride is now being added to bottled water as a "health benefit" which is absolutely insane. Fluoride is toxic, and you should try your best to avoid it going into your body in any facet. Once again we have been lied to! There is an entire organization fighting against fluoride exposure. The Fluoride Action Network is a group that fights against this very topic. According to their website, they are "an international coalition seeking to broaden public awareness about the toxicity of fluoride compounds and the health impacts of current fluoride exposure. Along with providing comprehensive and up-to-date information on fluoride issues to citizens, scientists, and policymakers alike, FAN remains vigilant in monitoring government agency actions that may impact the public's exposure to fluoride." [37] You can visit their website to learn more about this toxic issue at www.fluoridealert.org.

There are all sorts of amazing natural beauty products that actually work, smell good, and don't make you susceptible to disease. You just have to know about them and do your research. I even found mascara at Target that doesn't have parabens in it. It is all about knowing what to look for and becoming an educated consumer. If you have problems with acne, like I used to, switching from toxic skin and hair products, is essential. Ingredients like parabens and sulfates can actually cause acne and if you are already prone to that, it will increase the inflammation and the regularity of your breakouts. I learned this at 17 when I had a pizza face and was desperate to know why. I went to several dermatologists and my Mom spent thousands of dollars on facial peels, creams, lotions, and potions, to cure my acne. I did everything except go on Acutane, which I knew was toxic and deadly and I did not want it in my body, but nothing I did worked. When I started to learn about cleansing and toxicity everything changed. I began getting acupuncture regularly to clear the blocked energy in my body, and I began doing cleanses and taking herbs. I removed my toxic beauty products and replaced them with natural ones. Within the first month of doing this, my face was almost completely clear. Within six months, my acne was gone completely. I haven't had it since.

There are many ways to diminish toxins, but all of these are relatively easy. Like I said, some toxins we can't get away from, but we have the power to greatly diminish many of these harmful impurities in our life. If you are a mother, or if you are pregnant, it is essential to get these chemicals out of your home. You can find all natural baby products that do not contain these ingredients. Even when you are pregnant, if you put these chemicals on your skin it can soak in and affect the baby. Why not give your child the best fighting chance like we discussed earlier. An amazing natural moisturizer you can use for face cream and body lotion is organic coconut oil. I rubbed this on my stomach twice a day when I was pregnant and I did not get one stretch mark. It is also amazing for the face and to relieve dry skin.

I even purchase organic natural diapers and wipes for my daughter because most of the regular brands contain some of the ingredients we have been discussing. Most wipes have parabens and other toxic chemicals, and most diapers have chlorine and other toxic substances in them. Why? I don't know. Why do you think I am so ticked off about all of this? I do know I don't want these poisons on my baby, and I have a choice not to purchase these items. The best brand of all-natural non-toxic diapers I have found are from, the Honest Company started by celebrity actress Jessica Alba. I love the Honest diapers and her whole product line! She became angry by what these other companies where producing after she had her first child and took it upon herself to make a positive change. Talk about getting educated then empowered! I like to say she channeled her 'One Angry Chick' energy into making a beautiful company with fantastic products. To learn how to order these diapers visit your **ECEG**.

It all starts with a choice of wanting change. If you implement these simple steps to detoxifying your life, I can promise you that you will feel and look better, you will feel more empowered, and you will be making a difference. The more you know, the more you can help others know, and that is how we will affect change.

Chapter 6

Your Sacred Space

Your home is a place that is sacred. It is where you go for rest, shelter, and comfort. Yet, as I mentioned earlier, our homes have become toxic bubbles. There are many unseen toxins in our household that we cannot avoid, but there are also many that we can. Just like every other aspect of your life, there are things that are avoidable and those that are not. By being aware of these factors we can greatly diminish our exposure to things that are silently harming our families and us. The first order of business when you are detoxifying your home is to get rid of cleaning products that cause more harm than good. Most of the top label brands use a variety of chemicals and poisons that are unnecessary to get the job done. There are natural alternatives to bleaching agents, soap scum, stain removers, and detergents. There is a natural alternative for everything you have under the kitchen sink right now. We do not need to pollute our families or our environment to get our houses clean. We can do it naturally and ecologically. My daughters could ingest most of the cleaning products I use and they would not die from toxic poisoning. Not that I would want them to consume these things, but God forbid if they ever got into them, I am not that worried because they are not that toxic.

Have you ever stopped to think about what was in your dishwashing soap, or the detergent you use to wash your clothes? Most regular brands are very toxic, and unless you know what to look for, you are probably exposing your self to many harmful and potentially deadly chemicals when you eat off your plate or wear the clothes fresh out of the wash. Again, this sound like I am being paranoid, but it is really something very simple you can change to diminish your toxic exposure. Cleaning products of all kinds have been linked to cancers, autoimmune diseases, allergies, asthma, and skin conditions. I have know many people that when they clean up their living space and start to use organic natural products their allergies and other health issues start to vanish. There are literally thousands of toxic ingredients out there, but here is a list of certain standard ingredients that I recommend getting out of your home.

-Most All-Purpose Cleaners: These contain neurotoxins and chemicals that can irritate the nasal cavity. These can be absorbed through the skin or inhaled. Synthetic solvents can also cause hormone disruption.

-Butyl Cello solve (2-butoxyethanol, 2-butoxyethanol acetate or Ethylene glycol monobutyl ether) Butyl cello solve is a toxic glycol either chemical which can result in potential irritation and tissue damage from ingestion, inhalation, exposure through cuts or in the eyes. The general population is exposed to this through cleaning liquids. The annual production of this chemical exceeds 1 million pounds annually! Some of the issues associated with the ingestion of this chemical are breathing problems, low blood pressure, low hemoglobin levels, acidic blood, and blood in the urine.

-Formaldehyde is a preservative found in lots of household products. It is a carcinogen and even low levels of formaldehyde cause irritation of the eyes, nose, throat, and skin. If someone is asthmatic they may be more sensitive to the effects of this chemical. In laboratory studies, rats developed nose cancer from formaldehyde. This is also a common preservative found in most vaccines given to babies and young children.

-Automatic Dishwasher Detergents: Most of these have chlorine in them that is activated with the water. This can be released in the steam, leach onto dishes and can cause eye irritation if the dishwasher is opened

-Carpet Cleaners are extremely toxic especially for children. These fumes can cause cancer and liver damage. According to the Annual Report of the American Association of Poison Control Centers, Upholstery and Carpet cleaners accounted for 5,397 poison exposures in 2005 alone. The majority of these, exposures, over 3,500, involved children under 6. [37]

-Bleach: This common household chemical may cause reproductive, endocrine, and immune system disorder, according to the Annual Report of the American Association of Poison Control Centers' National Poisoning and Exposure Database [38].

-Degreasers: These contain petroleum distillates and butyl cello solve which can damage lung tissues and also dissolve fatty tissue around the nerve cell

-Drain Cleaners: These are one of the most hazardous products because they contain lye or sodium hydroxide that can cause severe damage to the eyes, skin, mouth, and stomach. These can be fatal if swallowed.

-Glass Cleaner: Ammonia is a main ingredient in most glass cleansers. These fumes can cause irritation to the eyes and respitory system. According to the American Association of Poison Control ammonia based glass cleaners accounted for 6,356 poison exposures (2005). Getting ammonia in the eyes can cause burns or even blindness. [38]

According to the Organic Consumers Association in their article "How Toxic Are Your Cleaning Products", they state that,

> "Cleaning ingredients vary in the type of health hazard they pose. Some cause acute, or immediate, hazards such as skin or respiratory irritation, watery eyes, or chemical burns, while others are associated

with chronic, or long-term, effects such as cancer. The most acutely dangerous cleaning products are corrosive drain cleaners, oven cleaners, and acidic toilet bowl cleaners, according to Philip Dickey of the Washington Toxics Coalition. Corrosive chemicals can cause severe burns on eyes, skin and, if ingested, on the throat and esophagus. Ingredients with high acute toxicity include chlorine bleach and ammonia, which produce fumes that are highly irritating to eyes, nose, throat and lungs, and should not be used by people with asthma or lung or heart problems. These two chemicals pose an added threat in that they can react with each other or other chemicals to form lung-damaging gases. Combining products that contain chlorine and ammonia or ammonia and lye (in some oven cleaners) produces chloramine gases, while chlorine combined with acids (commonly used in toilet bowl cleaners) forms toxic chlorine gas. Fragrances added to many cleaners, most notably laundry detergents and fabric softeners may cause acute effects such as respiratory irritation, headache, sneezing, and watery eyes in sensitive individuals or allergy and asthma sufferers. The National Institute of Occupational Safety and Health has found that one-third of the substances used in the fragrance industry are toxic. But because the chemical formulas of fragrances are considered trade secrets, companies aren't required to list their ingredients but merely label them as containing "fragrance." [39]

The article goes on to discuss how other ingredients in certain cleaners may have low acute toxicity as well. This can also contribute to long-term health effects, such as cancer or hormone disruption and birth defects. Some of the sudsing agents in these products, when combined with preservatives that are often present, can form carcinogens that can easily be absorbed by the skin. Many of these chemicals are neurotoxins and are suspected to cause damage to the brain and nervous system. These are definitely not substances that sound safe for anyone especially children.

There are lots of other toxic substances and products that increase your risk and exposure to deadly toxins and disease. These are just a few of the things that you may use everyday, without even knowing the effect it has on your life. Again my purpose of this information is to just give you a small look inside our lives, so we can see some of the things we may need to change in order to protect our health.

On a positive note, there are lots of companies out there that have great quality cleaning products that are safe for your home, your children, and the environment. One of the brands that I love is Begley's Best, created by Ed Begley Jr, who is a well-known environmental activist and actor. He has a great all purpose cleaner and stain remover that are non-toxic and safe for the environment. His products last forever and are affordably priced. You can purchase them online and at Whole Foods. For me it is about finding products that clean well, are environmentally friendly, and diminish my toxic exposure. While I can't control everything that is toxic, I can certainly try to in my home and on my body.

Chapter 7

Your Life Detoxed

After reading all this information, I can imagine that some of you may be feeling pretty overwhelmed or down at this moment. I assure you that my intention is not to create more stress in your already stress-filled life. My whole mission with this book, is for you to know that there is a better way, that there is a way through the darkness into a life of true health, natural healing, and balance. I don't know what that looks like for you exactly, but what I do know is that a new life is possible. Besides educating ourselves about our health, nutrition, and the world around us, it is just as important for you to educate yourself about your mind. I mentioned the power of the mind earlier in the story about Nicholas, but I want to go into a little more detail before we end our time together. I have always been fascinated by the human mind and the potential that it holds. I remember in college that I would just devour any of my psychology or communications home work because I was so interested in the way the brain worked. Yet, it wasn't until a few years later that I got really into personal growth that I started to find the answers I had always been searching for about the power that we all have within; the power of our minds.

NLP -Neural Linguistic Programming

From the ages of 21 until now, I devoured personal growth books. I have read everything from Wallace Wattles, to Napoleon Hill, to Tony Robins, to Stephen Covey, Paulo Cohelo, Marianne Williamson, and many more. Each time I would learn something new about myself whether it was a new way of thinking or something I wanted to change. I was introduced to a modality called NLP (Neural Linguistic Programming), and that shifted my focus even more on the discovery of how our minds work. Through the study of NLP I learned about why we have certain behaviors, fears, phobias, and goals. I learned about how our conscious and unconscious minds are mostly programmed to work against each other unless we go in and change some things around. Right away I started to connect the dots of how this works in our lives with our health. If we have a certain belief about health, food, or nutrition that conflicts with what our goal might be, then we will have a very hard time making the changes necessary to complete that goal. Most of the time these beliefs that we have are unconscious, and we don't even know we have them. For example, if your goal is to lose weight yet all you ever tell yourself is 'I can't lose weight no matter what I do', your subconscious mind will except that as truth and your body will follow its lead, thus never losing weight. It takes some time, and diligence to uncover the things that are holding us back. One of the hardest things in life is to look at ourselves and work on our weak spots. However, we are responsible for what is holding us back, nothing less, and nothing more. The minute we start to blame others or have a victim mentality that is the minute we give up our God given power!

My goal as Certified Master NLP Practitioner and Hypnotherapist, is to help people uncover these hidden truths so they can unlock their true potential, make better choices health wise, and start on a path to a new life. NLP is a way to actually detoxify the mind by literally replacing negative thoughts with positive ones, release old beliefs that aren't serving us, and rediscover who we really are. When I started my private practice, my intent was to create a safe haven for people to learn these techniques, get empowered with their own minds and bodies, and move forward into a brand new exciting life. Knowing that we live in a toxic world, is enough to stress any of us out, but the truth is, we can be the ones in control. We get to control our minds, therefore we get to control what we put in and on our bodies, and therefore, we get to control our health and our lives. The thing that I love about NLP is that it works quickly, if the person is ready for change. I do not believe it takes years of therapy or coaching to make substantial changes in one's life. I believe that if we really set our minds to something, we can change our life in one day, one second even, just by making a new decision. That new decision could be as easy as, 'I want to learn something new about my body today', or 'I want to drink more water', or whatever that may be.

By now you may be thinking that some of what we have talked about is too hard to do, to challenging to be aware of, or maybe you just don't know where to start. You might be thinking, well yeah this is easy for Brittney because she is healthy, was raised that way, and never had any health challenges. We have all been through our challenges in life; it is what we do after them that counts. I want to share a story with you of why I have chosen to be on this path now, and why I am so passionate about helping people detox their bodies and minds. This story was a pivotal moment in my life where I made a choice. I made a promise to myself that I have kept to this day, and it is what drives me to help people along this path. You see, we all have challenges, but we all have second chances at having a great life as well. This was mine.

When I was 13 years old I became addicted to drugs and alcohol. I started hanging out with a bad crowd, and with kids that were much older than I was. At that time in my life I was going through some challenges at home, and I was very angry with my parents. I don't know if any of you can relate to being mad at your parents, but I was. I wanted to rebel, and I didn't care who I hurt, especially myself. I started smoking cigarettes, pot, and drinking alcohol daily. At that time, which was the mid 90's, there were these illegal parties called Raves that were getting really popular. Raves were all night dance parties, usually in old abandon buildings or out in the desert, where kids would take a lot of drugs and dance all night to techno and house music. I thought these parties were the best things on the planet, and I became obsessed with going! Of course by this time I was only about 14 years old, so I would have to lie to my parents to go to them. I would say I was sleeping at a girlfriend's house then sneak out their bedroom window and have one of my older guy friends that drove pick me up. As I started to get more into the Rave scene my pallet for drugs increased. I started experimenting with hallucinogenic drugs like Acid and Ecstasy pills. These drugs would allow me to stay up all night dancing and feeling great. I also started testing out other drugs like speed and cocaine, although I didn't like those as much. Acid and Ecstasy was definitely my thing.

For those of you that know anything about these two drugs, they are both potentially brain damaging even after a single use. If something goes wrong or you get a bad batch, it can be over very quickly. I abused these drugs for several years, not thinking that I had any sort of problem. I even took Acid at school one day while I was in 10th grade, and none of my teachers knew! Because my home life was a bit of a mess I had convinced myself that I deserved to get high because I wanted to escape. Believe it or not I still ate really healthy at this time. I was still a vegetarian, and I thought I was counteracting the effects of the drugs with vitamins and other healthy supplements I was taking. I also still managed to get straight A's in school, so my parents didn't really know how bad my addictions were. By the time I was 16 I would have considered myself a full-blown drug addict. I had to get high on something everyday. I was up to smoking about a pack of cigarettes a day and I didn't even consider pot a drug anymore, so you know I was on a bad track. One summer night in June, my friends and I planned to go to a rave out in Barstow California, which is in the middle of the desert and about three hours from where I lived. Of course I lied to my Mom and told her I was staying over with a girlfriend. So off we went to the rave that was supposed to be the party of the year! I was so excited! We had all decided to do something called a "candy flip" that night which is when you combine Acid and Ecstasy. Because I had done these drugs so many times before, I had started to build up a tolerance to them. This night I took a lot of drugs! I don't remember how many hits of each I took, but I remember stopping at about five hits or so of each drug. On top of that, I was smoking pot, and I had been drinking alcohol earlier that day. Mind you, I weighed about 105 lbs at the time. What happened next was one of the worst experiences of my life.

After about an hour or so at the rave the drugs started to really kick in. Usually I always felt in control of the drugs, but that night they totally took over my body. I started to feel really sick and my body went numb. My heart started to beat out of my chest, and because I was on hallucinogens my vision was completely impaired. Not only could I not really see, but also what I was seeing was really scary. I was having what they call a bad trip. Everywhere I looked I saw demons, monsters, bugs, and weird things. I felt like I was losing control of my body and my mind. I couldn't think or focus, and I didn't really know where I was. Then my body started to shut down, or so I thought. At this point, I was curled up in a bathroom stall crying to my girlfriend that I was pooping and peeing all over myself. She kept telling me that I wasn't, but because I didn't have control over my body, I felt like I was constantly going to the bathroom on my clothes. I saw bugs crawling out of my skin and when I looked at myself in the mirror I looked like a demon. I thought I was going to die. At 16 years old my life would be over. At that point in time I knew I had lost control. There was still some part of my mind that was sane, and so I started to pray. I prayed to God for hours saying this phrase over and over again. "Please God give me my body and my mind back and I will never abuse it again. I will spend the rest of my life doing good things to it, I don't want to die, please help me!"

I repeated that in my head for hours until the drugs slowly started to wear off. By this time it was morning and the cops had started to break up the rave. I had curled myself up in a ball on a blanket that we had, and had been there for however long. My friends, who were also coming down off drugs helped me to the car and we all drove home. I remember sitting in the back seat, still completely out of it, and now in a lot of physical pain from the drugs. I just kept repeating that mantra in my mind. I was so scared that I was going to have brain damage or I had dramatically damaged my body in some way. I went home, didn't tell my parents, and slept for a good nine hours. When I woke up I made a pact to myself, and God, that I would never do drugs again, and one day help people live healthier lives. I have been sober from drugs ever since.

Because of that night, and because of what I went through, I started to get really into health. I started to cleanse my body and learn about different herbs and natural ingredients that could help reverse some of the damage I did to my cells. I do not think I would be on this path today had that not happened to me. I am so grateful that my life was spared, and that I made a decision to change. I am so grateful that I now have an opportunity to inspire others with my story and to help uplift them back into a place of empowerment. There are so many people out there battling addictions whether it is drugs, or foods, or other things. I want every person to know that is battling an addiction or knows someone that is, that a new life is possible! Miracles can happen, and you can have a better life. Your body is a miracle, and I believe it can over come anything as long as your mind is on board.

Now that I am a mother I can't even imagine what I put my Mom through when I was battling addiction. I know what it is like on the other side now, and it is horrible to watch someone go through that. I have watched several close family members battle horrible drug addictions. At times I felt hopeless because they didn't want help yet, but we each must find our own paths. All one can do is hope and pray that people will realize their true potential and the miracle their body really is.

Hope For the Future

Health is so multifaceted as we have been discussing. My vision for this world is for all of us to embrace our power both mentally and physically so we can become the beacons of light we were meant to be. The foods that we put in our body, the products we use, the language we speak in, and the people we surround ourselves with all have an effect on the type of life we will lead and live. I know that each one of you is amazing no matter where you are at right now in your life. You can change, you can heal, and you can over come any obstacle you are facing. I hope that I have inspired you to take a closer look at your health, your life, and the many choices you have. I hope you choose the *One Angry Chick* way, and become empowered and educated. I hope you fight against this *Silent Scandal* and make more people aware of the topics in this book. I hope you use your **ECEG** to learn more and do your research. I hope that you take time everyday to be grateful for your body and your life.

Together we can make change for ourselves and for future generations. We may not agree on everything that has been discussed in this book, but I hope that we agree on one thing. Life is a precious gift. WE have a choice each day when we wake up to start over, to start fresh, and to make our dreams a reality. In order to do that, we must have our health. Together lets take this world from toxic, to empowered, and be the change that we want to see! From my family to yours, I wish you all the health, love, and abundance in the world.

Connect with Brittney

Website: www.yourlifedetoxed.com

Blog: http://www.brittneykara.wordpress.com

Face book: http://facebook.com/brittneykara

Twitter: http://twitter.com/brittneykara

CopyRight 2011 Brittney Kara All Rights Reserved

Educated Consumers Empowerment Guide (ECEG)

Please use this information to expand your knowledge, heal your body, and spread the TRUTH.

Be Blessed, Be Healthy, Be Free,

Brittney Kara (aka. One Angry Chick)

Resources For Your Health:

1. Structured water
www.VortexWaterTech.com

2. Cleansing, Super foods and Supplements
www.besttotalbodycleanse.com

3. Best Natural Health Products for cooking
www.bragg.com

4. Best Health News:
- www.naturalnews.com
- www.drmercola.com
- www.isagenixhealth.net
- www.organicconsumers.org
- www.fooddemocracynow.org

5. Best Health Blogs:
Messages From Your Body - www.brittneykara.wordpress.com
Food Babe- www.foodbabe.com
Green Smoothie Girl - www.greensmoothiegirl.com

6. Don't be a GMO- Learn More!!
- www.justlabelit.org
- www.nongmoproject.org/learn-more/what-is-gmo/
- http://gmo.mercola.com/

Resources For Your Education:

Documentaries:

Food Inc - www.takepart.com/foodinc

Food Matters- www.foodmatters.tv/

Forks Over Knives - www.forksoverknives.com/

Processed People- www.processedpeople.com/

-The Greater Good - www.greatergoodmovie.org/

-Genetic Roulette- www.geneticroulettemovie.com/

-Thrive - www.thrivemovement.com/

Books:

(This is a small list as to not overwhelm you. It is just a good sample of some of the amazing books on health and empowerment out there)

Miracle Super Foods That Heal- Dr Tony O'Donnell

Instant E.N.E.R.G.Y- Dr Marilyn Joyce

The China Study- T.Colin Campbell

The Omnivore's Dilemma: A Natural History of Four Meals- Michael Pollan

Skinny Bitch- Rory Freedman and Kim Barnoin

The Have It All Woman- Susan Sly

Resources For Your Home/Family

1. The Honest Company- www.honest.com

2. Bagley's Best- www.begleysbest.com

References:

1. The Center For Disease Control (CDC)
http://www.cdc.gov/exposurereport/reportresults.htm/

2. EWG Study on Newborns
http://www.ewg.org/reports/bodyburden2

3. Death by Medicine Study- By Gary Null, PhD; Carolyn Dean MD, ND; Martin Feldman, MD; Debora Rasio, MD; and Dorothy Smith, PhD
http://www.webdc.com/pdfs/deathbymedicine.pdf

4. Natural News
http://www.naturalnews.com/009278_prescription_drugs_counterthink.html

5. Death By Medicine Study -By Gary Null, PhD; Carolyn Dean MD, ND; Martin Feldman, MD; Debora Rasio, MD; and Dorothy Smith, PhD
http://www.eurekaencyclopedia.com/index.php/Category:Death_by_Medicine

6. The Nutrition Institute of America Study
http://www.stopcancer.com/medicalmistakes.htm

7. "An Ancient Cure for Modern Life," Yoga Journal, Jan/Feb 2002- Alison Rose Levy
http://www.yogajournal.com/health/647

8. Dr. F. Batmanghelidj
http://www.watercure.com/

9. CDC High Blood Pressure Statistics
http://www.cdc.gov/bloodpressure/facts.htm

10. Natural News
http://www.naturalnews.com/040026_Nestle_water_supply_domination.html

11. Pharmacy Times
http://www.pharmacytimes.com/publications/issue/2010/May2010/RxFocusTopDrugs-0510

12. Miracle Super Foods That Heal by Dr. Tony O'Donnell PG 114-116

13. The Cancer Business by Patrick Rattigan ND
http://www.theforbiddenknowledge.com/hardtruth/cancer_business.htm

14. An Oasis of Healing Cancer Center
http://www.anoasisofhealing.com/our-program/target-eliminate-cancer/intravenous-vitamin-c/#axzz2RbaGpmmN

15. The Cancer Tutor
http://www.cancertutor.com/Cancer/Laetrile.html

16. EPA- Children and Cancer
http://www.epa.gov/ace/ace3draft/draft_pdfs/ACE3ChildhoodCancerReviewPackage3-02-11.pdf

17. Ron Gdanski " Childhood Cancer Epidemic"
http://www.alive.com/articles/view/17075/childhood_cancer_epidemic

18. Mayo Clinic - "Can Curcumin Slow Cancer"
http://www.mayoclinic.com/health/curcumin/AN01741

19. CDC Vaccine Schedule
http://www.cdc.gov/vaccines/schedules/easy-to-read/child.html

20. CDC Autism Statistics
http://www.cdc.gov/features/autismprevalence/

21. Infant Deaths
http://www.vaccinetruth.org/vaccine_deaths.htm

22. The International Medical Council on Vaccination
http://www.vaccinationcouncil.org/about/

23. Super Size Me Facts
http://www.vivavegie.org/101book/text/nolink/social/super-sizeme.htm

24. GMO Labeling
http://justlabelit.org/right-to-know/labeling-around-the-world/

25. Aspartame study
http://www.medicalnewstoday.com/releases/34040.php

26. Mercola on Monsanto
http://articles.mercola.com/sites/articles/archive/2010/10/23/monsanto-finally-reaping-its-just-desserts.aspx

27. The Dirty Dozen
http://www.organic.org/articles/showarticle/article-214

28. Dr Mercola "Best and Worst Fruits and Vegetables"
http://articles.mercola.com/sites/articles/archive/2010/11/29/recommended-vegetable-list.aspx

29. Dr Kradjian- Milk Letter
http://www.notmilk.com/kradjian.html

30. Peta's Milk research
http://www.peta.org/issues/animals-used-for-food/cows-milk-a-cruel-and-unhealthy-product.aspx

31. http://www.peta.org/issues/animals-used-for-food/vegan-children-healthy-and-happy.aspx

32. Natural News-Cow's Milk allergies
http://www.naturalnews.com/010443_cows_milk_asthma.html

33. Cornucopia Study on Carrageenan
http://www.cornucopia.org/wp-content/uploads/2013/02/Carrageenan-Report1.pdf

34. Scripts Study on food and drugs
http://www.scripps.edu/news/press/2010/20100329.html

35. Times Magazine- "How the First Nine Months Shape Your Life" by Anne Murphy Paul
http://www.time.com/time/magazine/article/0,9171,2021065,00.html

36. Natural News- Soda Pop Industry
http://www.naturalnews.com/030550_soda_pop_advertising.html

37. Fluoride Action Network
http://www.fluoridealert.org/about/

38. American Association of Poison Control
http://www.aapcc.org/

39. Organic Consumers Association-How Toxic Are Your Cleaning Supplies
http://www.organicconsumers.org/articles/article_279.cfm